I am so grateful to Rebecca for sharing this heartfelt, life-giving resource. These pages are full of surprising lessons, wisdom and deeper understanding of God's care and promises learned during the loss of her wonderful husband Scott. In whatever way loss comes and "life never looks the same again," the reader will gain strength for the journey, hope and fresh vitality to once again flourish in life.

Catherine Hart Weber, Ph.D.
Counselor, Life Coach, Teacher
Author, *Flourish: Discover Vibrant Living*

As a pastor who has ministered to innumerable, but individually precious people pierced with grief, it is with practical as well as personal joy to witness the publication of Rebecca Bauer's *Life Beyond Grief*—foremost, because it unfolds a *practical pathway of hope and comfort* which will bring healing to any who grieve the passing of a loved one. And *personally,* it is meaning filled because I observed the author living through the sudden loss of her husband.

More than an intense story, here is the graciously sensitive, helpfully comforting and spiritually discerning outcome. It frames a work which my pastoral sense tells me will become a source of stabilizing hope born of God-given wisdom.

Dr. Jack W. Hayford
Chancellor, The King's University

Life After Grief is refreshing, authentic, and will speak to the hearts of readers. Rebecca's husband's death—10 years ago now—was a profound event in her life. With this powerful "credential," she writes with clear understanding, dividing her thoughts into instructive categories: choices, wrestling, lessons and application. The experiences she shares from her own journey are focused, insightful and practical, and this book is filled with concrete tips for not only surviving the road of mourning, but thriving along the way. In *Life After Grief*, readers will find comfort, direction and support as they travel their own journey through grief.

Ray Mitsch
Author, *Grieving the Loss of Someone You Love*

The Hayford family has been dear to me for many years, and Rebecca's story is close to my heart. As she shares how the sudden loss of her husband changed her life, she conveys a very emotional subject with grace, honesty and practicality. If you've experienced grief on any level or are trying to support someone who's going through a difficult time, *Life After Grief* is for you.

Robert Morris
Founding Senior Pastor, Gateway Church
Bestselling Author, *The Blessed Life, From Dream to Destiny* and *The God I Never Knew*

LIFE AFTER GRIEF

Life &After Grief

REBECCA
HAYFORD BAUER

Regal

For more information and
special offers from Regal Books, email us at
subscribe@regalbooks.com

Published by Regal
From Gospel Light
Ventura, California, U.S.A.
www.regalbooks.com
Printed in the U.S.A.

Library of Congress Cataloging-in-Publication Data
Bauer, Rebecca Hayford.
Life after grief: choosing the path to healing / Rebecca Hayford Bauer.
pages cm
ISBN 978-0-8307-6783-0 (trade paper)
1. Grief—Religious aspects—Christianity. 2. Loss (Psychology)—Religious aspects—
Christianity. 3. Bereavement—Religious aspects—Christianity. I. Title.
BV4909.B39 2014
248.8'66—dc23
2013031691

To "The Sisterhood"

*There are many sisters in the Body of Christ who faithfully walked
my journey with me, and I am forever thankful to all of you. There were also
many brothers who prayed me through. But it was the sisters who walked me
through and talked me through—for almost five years—while I learned who
I was in this new life I had stepped into. I can never thank you enough,
and you will recognize your part in my story as you read through this book.
All of our stories are here!*

There are two, however, whom I wish to specifically name:

*To my sister, Christa:
Thank you for always being there. You were my rock.
You brought prayer, support, light and laughter
(and occasionally chocolate!)
while I walked a very dark journey.*

*To my sister-in-law, Cathy:
You walked the journey of loss long before I did.
Thank you for being an example of how to graciously walk the road.
Your encouragement forward by word and example
has been invaluable.*

CONTENTS

PART 3—THE HARD WORK OF GRIEF:
WALKING THROUGH THE TUNNEL

PART 4—BUILDING A NEW LIFE:
STEPPING INTO THE LIGHT

PART 5—THE COLORS OF GRACE

FOREWORD

On December 28, 2012, our youngest child Robin stepped into the presence of Jesus after fiercely battling cancer for several years. Throughout her journey we continually sought answers, prayed fervently and believed God for her healing. We were heartbroken, though we know she experienced the ultimate healing. There truly is no way to describe this kind of heartache. But for the grace and mercy of our heavenly Father and the loving support of family and friends, we would not have been able to stand the pain of it.

Rebecca Bauer's dad, Pastor Jack Hayford, was one of the first friends to reach out to us with prayer and comfort. He knew the journey we were experiencing and shared with us a beautiful vision he had of Robin's entrance into heaven.

In October 2003, Jack's son-in-law (Rebecca's husband, Scott) died of a brain aneurysm. Scott and Rebecca were pastoring The Church on the Way at the time, so Rebecca's work and living situation changed immediately. At the same time, all of her children were getting married, so within a three-year period, her house was completely emptied.

Rebecca beautifully outlines her journey through the "valley of the shadow of death" (see Ps. 23:4). This book will be a wonderful, practical help to anyone who has experienced the loss of a loved one, a marriage, a business or a dream. When does the grieving end? How can you get through it? Where do you even start?

You might be asking, "Where is God in *my* situation?" We can quickly answer: He is with you. He is holding your heart and will continue to as long as you have breath. In Jesus' first message in the synagogue, we find great comfort in the words He quoted from Isaiah: "He has sent me to bind up the broken-hearted" (see Isa. 61:1; Luke 4:18). Indeed, He does . . . and we join Rebecca, seeking to do the same.

In the year since our daughter's passing, we have learned that when your heart is broken beyond anything you could ever imagine, only a miracle of God can bring the necessary healing. Just as with the physical healing of broken bones or bleeding wounds, it is a process that requires time, the balm of Gilead and the healing oil that only the Holy Spirit can provide.

These words from Lamentations are still relevant today: "Surely my soul remembers and is bowed down within me. This I recall to my mind, Therefore I have hope. The LORD'S loving-kindnesses indeed never cease, for His compassions never fail. They are new every morning; Great is Your faithfulness" (Lam. 3:20-23, *NASB*).

Whatever difficulty you are facing, remember: God promises He will never leave you or forsake you (see Deut. 31:6). As you read the pages of this book, may God speak to you, comfort you with His loving presence and abundantly provide for every need.

James and Betty Robison
Cohosts, *LIFE Today* television program,
Fort Worth, Texas

Part 1

BEGINNING THE JOURNEY: HOW TO USE THIS BOOK

If you've picked up this book, chances are that either you are in the middle of a grief journey or you know someone who is. I want to provide an overview of how to use this book, but first, may I offer my heartfelt condolences and prayer that the Lord will—as I'm sure He already has—give you strength for the journey and provide His comfort day by day, and moment by moment.

My goal in writing is simple: I want to share the lessons that God taught me on my journey of loss and grief—because many were completely different from what I expected. While I will never minimize the sorrow, tears and difficulty of walking the road of loss, I found that the lessons the Lord taught me opened a door to my future, taught me how to see life with fresh vitality, and shaped me into a bolder, more secure person.

I learned a lot about God, too. Though I had followed the Lord all my life, I had to wrestle anew with what I believed about Him and about His Word. My view of salvation was never an issue, but I wrestled with my view of God's involvement in my life. Was He as concerned about me as I had been taught? Would He really take me "from glory to glory" as His Word said (2 Cor. 3:18)? Was Jesus really the high priest who could "sympathize with our weaknesses" (Heb. 4:15)? In other words, did He *really* know? And did He *really* care? I would like to share some of my "wrestlings" with you, because what I found was that God not only cared, but also *knew* what I suffered more than I had ever suspected. He had walked the journey of suffering and loss before I did, and He was fully prepared to walk my journey with me. I also came to a deeper understanding that the promises He made in His Word really were true!

As I thought about how best to share these lessons with you, I decided to divide each chapter of the book into five sections:

Choices: One of the surprises of my journey was how often I discovered that I had choices about *how* I was going to grieve, and how I was going to rebuild my future. I had the choice of joy or sorrow, life or death, faith or doubt—to name just a few! The sections titled "Choices" will each present a question and a choice that was made along the way.

Wrestling: In the psalms, David talked about "meditating" on God's Word and works, but Jacob described his encounter with God as "wrestling" (Gen. 32:24-25). Jacob's term better described the upheaval I experienced because *life wasn't turning out the way I thought it was supposed to.* I had always believed that God promised me a future and a hope. I believed that obedience to His Word and ways would bring blessing. Suddenly, that wasn't where I

found myself, and I wondered if I really still believed all o
things in the same way (and with the same expectancy) as
before? These sections will chronicle some of those wrestli
and tell about what I learned in the Bible.

Lesson: The lessons described are the ways that the "choices"
and "wrestlings" are practically lived out. We can learn amazing
truths in God's Word—and even feel comforted in our emotions
and strengthened in our spirits—but living them out requires
intentional application and specific, defined steps. When I faced
challenges, depression or a very tear-filled day, what difference
did knowing God's Word make? How should my life look when I
was walking with Jesus through the Valley of the Shadow? These
sections are intended to answer some of those questions.

Application: These sections provide practical steps that are
necessary to take on the road of loss. How do you process the paperwork and sort through the loved one's belongings? How do
you set parameters for your new life? How do you put finances in
order if you've never done that before? What are the accountabil-
ity points that need to be put into place? And how do you learn
to dream again when life will never, ever be the same? Of course,
I speak from my story of loss, which was being widowed, but
there are other losses,[1] and I trust that the "applications" will
offer concepts that can be used in your situation as well.

Interaction: The interactions are, for lack of a better term,
"activities." (My daughter jokingly called them my "adult-daycare
projects"!) These are things I did that helped keep me "forward
focused" (an easily remembered phrase that reminded me *every
day* that I was *choosing* to move forward). I am a very visual person, and some of these actually turned into art projects! (See
page 199.) The fact is that in the process of doing something

ver thinking" or "over feeling" the situa-
t of definition, understanding and "next
surface.

these
had
gs

17

Note
1. Though my loss was a death, and I will be using my own story throughout the book,
    I will be defining "loss" as *anything* that happens and "life never looks the same
    again." (See p. 23.) Further, keep in mind that some losses can be positive: To step
    through new doors in life, we always have to leave something behind. Graduations,
    weddings and births are all wonderful! And yet, life will never be the same again,
    and there are things we must let go of as we step into the future. There are goodbyes
    to be said at graduation, never living at Mom and Dad's again following a wedding,
    and priorities that change with the birth of a child. Every time I see a young mom
    with two or three children pulling on her, I remember the "loss" of never being alone!

1

THE FIRST CHOICE

Choices: The First Choice

Years after the death of my husband, someone asked me an interesting question:

If you could, would you go back?

I couldn't answer for a few minutes. Years of a long and horrible journey spun through my mind. I felt like Dorothy in *The Wizard of Oz*—I had faced the displacement and disorientation of suddenly being picked up and dropped in a new place. I had walked a very long journey, and, doggone it, I think I had faced those scary flying monkeys, too!

And I had overcome.

Would I go back?

I paused a minute before I answered, and as I considered, the answer became longer and longer. First, it's a pointless question to ask. We can't go back, and all of the wishing in the world won't make it so. Second, if I *could* go back, I would've done so the minute after Scott died. I wouldn't have waited years to make that decision. Third, it's asking the wrong question. The question to ask isn't, "Would you go back?" but, "Would you have picked this road?"

The answer to that is, "No." I would never have picked this road. I can't imagine anyone *choosing* to walk this awful journey.

But once we're on this road (and we *can't* go back), how we process the journey becomes our choice in many respects. As I walked my path of loss and grief, I found that the Lord presented me with a number of questions that helped me to continue to choose . . . well . . . *Life*.

I'll be the first to admit that "choosing life" actually made me downright mad in those first days and months following Scott's death. *Life* as I knew it had died, and *choosing life* flew in the face of the grief I felt, the hole I wanted to sit in, and the confusion I felt about what life was even *supposed* to look like now.

Our culture has made the phrase "choose life" a politically incorrect term, but the truth is that the original offer to choose life was presented by God thousands of years ago. In fact, the choice between life and death is *the* choice of Scripture. From the first couple's decision to choose the tree that brought death (see Gen. 2:16-17 and 3:22) rather than the tree of life, the Bible repeatedly offers the opportunity for choosing God's way—*the way of life*.

> I have set before you life and death, blessing and cursing; therefore choose life (Deut. 30:19).

> The fear of the LORD is a fountain of life, to turn one away from . . . death (Prov. 14:27).

"Get yourselves a new heart and a new spirit. For why should you die?" . . . says the Lord GOD. "Therefore turn and live!" (Ezek. 18:31-32).

We know that we have passed from death to life (1 John 3:14).

My "offer to choose life" began on December 1, 2003. Scott had died about five weeks before, and it definitely wasn't looking like it was going to be a happy holiday. I woke up that morning and, as my feet hit the floor, I sensed the Lord challenging me with the words:

Today I want you to choose life.

I knew what the challenge was: The Lord was calling me to refuse the sting of death in my life. I also knew that the way to do that was to do the things that contributed to building a future. It was Christmastime, so those things would be:

Putting up lots of lights!

Decorating everything!

Sending out Christmas cards!

Christmas shopping for my kids!

I did it. It felt like just motions at the time, yet I knew I was making a choice: I was choosing life. I was choosing to rest in the life-givingness of Jesus' coming like I never had before. And I have been choosing life on my journey ever since then.

Would I go back?

All of these thoughts flashed through my mind as I pondered the question. In all honesty, it's difficult to consider going back now that God has had me on a forward-focused, life-choosing road for years!

So my answer to the person who asked was:

> *I would never have chosen this journey—*
> *would never have chosen this road. But on this road,*
> *I have found that I know Jesus better, I have a life I love,*
> *and I like who I've become. I wouldn't have chosen this*
> *road, but what I've learned on this road has made the*
> *journey worth it.*

In the face of death and loss, choosing life made all the difference.

I have found that choosing life when you are walking through loss is never easy. It is so much easier to retreat into the darkness of the Valley of the Shadow; easier to stay in the cave; easier to mentally live in the past—and I had those moments, too. Jesus understands them. In fact, He said, "Difficult is the way which leads to life" (Matt. 7:14). You see, choosing life has to do with more than salvation; it also has to do with the choices we make every day—no matter what that day may hold. The good news is that Jesus has promised that He is "the resurrection and the life" (John 11:25).

Wherever you are on your journey of loss, and whatever your loss has entailed, can I invite you to accept His offer of life? I can promise that He will walk with you unto resurrection—resurrection of life, resurrection of newness, and resurrection of a future and a hope. But it starts by making the choice for life. If you make that choice, and walk this road with your hand in Jesus' hand, you too will be able to say:

I know Him better.
    I love my life.
        I like who I have become.

Wrestling: Enlarging Definitions

If there's anything I have learned in my grief process, it's that everyone's journey is different—a different circumstance, a different loss, a different process through the pain. Throughout our lives, each person will suffer loss. Unless our loss is exactly the same as someone else's, however, we have a difficult time finding the support and sympathy we need and long for. In fact, I've found that when our loss is different from someone else's, not only do we have difficulty finding comfort, but we do a pretty poor job of offering comfort as well

The inability to find and to give comfort ultimately comes down to the fact that we actually "rate" loss. *We judge loss in terms of what would be loss to us.* If we don't think that the kind of loss someone else has experienced would impact us, we treat it as though it is insignificant.

Let me offer a very simple example. Suppose a three-year-old picks a dandelion and brings it to you, insisting that it be used as tonight's centerpiece. You already know that, even with water, tomorrow it will be a withered weed. Before the loss ever occurs, the dandelion has been placed in two wildly differing value systems: weed vs. centerpiece. The next morning, of course, the child is devastated, and doesn't understand what happened. If you're like most of us, you move on with the day, and neglect to stop to help a three-year-old cry his or her tears.

What happened here? "Loss" was placed in a value system, and therefore the emotional need of the individual was neither acknowledged nor validated. As simple an illustration as this is, it highlights two important points:

> *Whatever the loss, to be truly comforted, (1) we need*
> *to have our loss valued for how we value it, and*
> *(2) we need to have the depth of our grief validated so*
> *that we can give expression to what has happened.*

Of course, the ultimate Comforter is God. But He also works through His people. In order for us to partner in both receiving and giving comfort, I would like for us to look at a bigger definition of loss, because it comes in a lot of different packages. Consider:

- a divorce
- a job loss
- betrayal by a friend
- marital infidelity
- the loss of a home through either financial reasons or disaster
- bankruptcy
- death—of a parent, a spouse, a child or a friend

We would probably all be sympathetic to those losses. But now consider these:

- the individual who, in the fifth grade, became the target of bullies at school when his or her family moved across country
- the woman facing haunting pain, grief or guilt following an abortion (even if she had the abortion before

she knew Christ, we rarely forgive, let alone comfort, someone who has experienced this type of loss)

- the woman who, following a divorce, is now a single mom trying to raise and support her kids
- the man who, following a divorce, now only sees his kids a few days a month
- the person who has been kicked out of an academic program (for whatever reason—some are fair; some are not)
- someone who has lost a pet (I used to be very uncompassionate toward this kind of loss—until a dog became "who I lived with")
- a person who has realized that a long-cherished dream will never come true
- an older person who is losing mobility and independence
- someone who has been put into hospice
- the person who was "left at the altar"
- someone who has "compounded" grief due to multiple losses in a short period of time
- people dealing with loss of health—their own or the agonizing process of watching a loved one deteriorate

This list could go on indefinitely, but the point is that loss happens all the time in all kinds of ways. I finally came up with this definition: "Loss is when anything happens and *life never looks the same again.*"

That is a big definition, and it happened to me. My husband died . . . and my life has never looked the same again. There was always an empty seat at the table. There was no one to hold hands with. He wasn't there to give our daughter away at her wedding. He wasn't there when any of our grandchildren were born. I missed his wisecracks during movies. I missed making red cabbage for him just because he liked it. I missed the TV being tuned to the Golf Channel. From the largest things to the smallest things—*life looked different*.

Loss.

The flip side of this discussion is the temptation to make the loss too large. Don't get me wrong here. Losses are certainly overwhelming—but in the middle of grief, it's easy to allow our loss to become all-consuming. Jesus said that He has overcome the world, and we limit ourselves from the start if we make our loss bigger than He is. This is one of the first concepts that the Lord pressed into my heart as I began my journey.

I had gone out for a walk. I had to move. I had to get out of the all-too-empty house. I had to get some air.

"Lord, I've lost everything," I said through tears.

Immediately, the words whispered into my heart were: "No, you haven't."

I was taken aback. And I was angry—angry that God wasn't defining things the way I was: Life as I knew it was over. *Over!*

At the same time, I knew what He meant: I hadn't lost my family. Or my home. Or my church. Or my salvation or mission or call or purpose. I hadn't lost *Him*.

As I look back on that moment, I understand that God was pressing me to define the loss within the parameters of:

> *what He was capable of dealing with,*
> > *what He was capable of doing in me, and*
> > > *what He was capable of redeeming.*

Jesus was already beginning to lead me *forward*. Just days into the journey, He was pressing me forward to a new life, a new future and a new hope. These were only beginning steps, and the journey would be long. But I still had Jesus . . . and *He's* everything.

Lesson: Three Stages of Grief

I think I expected grief to be a long hike through waist-deep mud. Rather, I found that it was more like standing waist-deep in the water at the beach in heavy surge. The assault was constant, but it came in waves. And like waves, they varied in their intensity. Sometimes I was standing in the ocean and, seeing a wave on its way, could brace for it. Other times it was like having my back to a tsunami—and all of a sudden being smashed flat and drowning.

As time went by, the waves progressively got smaller. In other words, there were more tsunamis at the beginning; a year or so in, they were fewer and less forceful. After five years, I felt like I was standing on the shore with the waves lapping at my feet. The loss—and the recognition of how it has altered my life— never completely leaves. I don't think this is necessarily a "bad" thing; the loss-event did change life and it did change me. A decade later, I still think of Scott every day. The difference is that now those thoughts generally come not with weeping, but rather with thanksgiving for the decades the Lord allowed him to be in my life.

Traditional Stages of Grief

Like waves, many talk about "the stages of grief." Typically, these stages will be presented as denial, anger, bargaining, depression—and, finally, acceptance. I've dealt with all of these stages on my journey, though I have found that there is no set time frame or order to them. There are even a couple of them that I may have dealt with more than once!

I once heard someone scoff at these stages, saying, "How can you 'deny' that someone is dead?" Admittedly, it's hard to deny that someone has died. But you *can* deny that life has changed. You *can* pretend that everything is the same in a desperate attempt to avoid acknowledging the reality of your loss. Why do you think that people try to (for example) keep all of the family celebrations exactly the same as Mom did them, even though Mom has been gone for years? Why do you think that people don't change someone's office? Or re-decorate? Or change the letterhead? Why do you think God had to remind Joshua that Moses was dead (see Josh. 1:2)? Because this desire to keep everything the same has always been true of humankind. None of us likes to face loss . . . or change.

My Time-Stages of Grief

Along the way, while I dealt with the emotional stages of grief described above, I observed my own stages of grief, primarily defined by time: shock (the first 100 days), survival (the first 6 months), and "the hard work of grief" (the first 2 years). Somewhere within that 6- to 24-month time frame, most people will have fully processed their loss. Some will go a bit faster, some a bit slower. My journey, before stepping back into the light, took about two and a half years. So no angst here. There is no buzzer that goes off at "23 months, 6 days, 18 minutes, 43 seconds," and now you're expected to be "all well." The journey through the Valley of the Shadow takes different lengths of time for different people.

The First 100 Days

For the first 100 days following Scott's death, I was in shock. There is no other way to describe it. I've had people whose loss was not sudden tell me that this stage felt different for them—they saw the loss coming and braced for it. It doesn't make the journey easier—just different. For me, life completely changed in a 24-hour period. I then found myself counting. Not in weeks. Not in months. I counted in days. "It's been 10 days since my husband died." "It's been 42 days since my husband died." "It's been 76 days . . ." "It's been 88 days . . ." Somehow when the days hit triple digits, something changed inside of me and I began counting in months. I still felt overwhelmed, but the shock was wearing off.

The First Six Months

Things were more stable by the six-month mark. I knew what my new job was. I knew where my new home was. I had paid bills by now. (Don't roll your eyes! My husband had been an economics major in college, and he took care of all of the financial stuff.) By the six-month mark, I had switched the accounts to my name. By then, adrenaline had waned. That adrenaline had allowed me to get a lot done (and there was a lot to do), but it also allowed me to sleep only two hours at a time. After six months, I pictured myself as no longer flailing in the middle of the ocean, about to drown, or under a tsunami. Now I was lying on the beach—I was on solid ground. I had survived. I was still dripping wet, freezing cold, and gasping for air. I still had a long way to go, but drowning was no longer a threat.

The First Two Years

I was now ready for the next stage of the process: "the hard work of grief." This stage was more intentional, though still sorrowful.

I began to view grief as my "job," and I had a stated goal: *to come out of this with the least amount of baggage possible.* (See p. 69.) This "hard work" took about two more years for me. But one morning I woke up and realized that I could actually see the light at the end of the tunnel, and I was ready to build a new life.

I share this time frame not to discourage you, but to encourage you when the journey seems long. It *is* long. Don't rush through it. Take the time you need and process everything so that you can come through "baggage free" and ready for your future. Our culture does a poor job of allowing people the time they need to walk the entire walk. We all want it to be done in a 30-minute show, or a 10-minute microwave dinner. But after you have walked the journey, you, too, will wake up and realize that you *really are* at the end of the tunnel, and you are stepping into the light again!

Application: A Word to the Comforters

Having to walk the road of grief and loss showed me how little I actually knew of it. So many times I had sought to comfort others, and, in retrospect, now realize how little comfort I actually had to offer. That is not to discourage you from offering help and comfort. Believe me . . . I could never have walked that journey without the Body of Christ coming alongside me so many times. *Please offer comfort!* But also please allow me to offer you a few guidelines to consider:

1. We all feel compelled to say something! I have chuckled over the statement made by one of Job's comforters: "My anxious thoughts make me answer . . ."

(Job 20:2). *Yeah. I've done that, too!* Many of the words we offer in our anxious attempts to comfort are not actually all that helpful. On my journey, I found that there were four things that truly comforted me:

- *"I love you."* The apostle Paul writes simply, "Love edifies" (1 Cor. 8:1). If we go to one another speaking words of love, we will always build up the other person. In Philippians 1:9, Paul says, "This I pray, that your love may abound still more and more in knowledge and all discernment." We need all of that—love, knowledge, discernment—when we go to comfort someone.

- *"I'm so sorry."* Scripture exhorts us to "weep with those who weep" (Rom. 12:15), but we're not usually comfortable with that activity. We want to "fix" the problem, not weep over it. Can you imagine a doctor telling a patient how to set his or her own leg rather than in compassion doing what needed to be done? In the case of loss, compassion and sympathy go a long way.

- *"I'm praying for you."* Colossians 1:9 encourages us to "not cease to pray" for one another. Too often I found that people wanted to tell me what they felt impressed to pray about for me instead of actually praying for me. Believe me when I say . . . the prayers of the Body of

Christ are what got me through every day for a very long time.

- *A memory of Scott.* In the days following his death, I heard some of the sweetest stories about Scott from different people in our congregation. Touchingly, one lady signed off her "memory note" by saying, "When I get to heaven, I want to hear Jesus say to me, 'Well done.' *Then* I want to hear my pastor say to me, 'I'm proud of you.'"

2. It helped when people allowed me to guide the conversation. There are things about grief that I never knew before . . . For instance, there is physical pain attached to it. Or sometimes my ears would literally shut down. I could see people's mouths moving, but I could no longer distinguish their words. When people came to me with their own agendas, it was always harder. I found that people tended to want to *tell* me things, rather than *ask* me things. Let the bereaved guide the conversation . . . because they know what they can handle. And keep in mind that, because each day in the process is different (especially early on), what was okay to talk about one time may not be okay the next time. Take your cues from the person you have come to comfort.

3. The grieving process takes longer than we think. Since having walked this road, I now put reminders on my calendar to call people who are on a journey of loss. Life moves on quickly for those who have not

suffered the loss; it can move incredibly slowly for those who are in the midst of it. Two weeks after my loss, when most others were moving on with their lives, it became really lonely. The calls, cards and letters I received later in the process let me know there were still people walking with me. As comforters, we need to remember to keep the bereaved close in our hearts, in our prayers, and in actual contact. Texts and emails count, by the way. These kinds of communication actually give the person "space," while still letting them know that others are bearing them up in prayer. Provide your phone number in case they want or need to talk.

4. Be patient with the bereaved person's desire to control. When my husband passed away, life felt so out of control that I kept trying to micro-manage my calendar. I kept the house over-neat. A friend who was widowed years before me went out and bought artificial plants and got rid of all of the real ones in her house. I've come to recognize that what may look like unusual behavior is actually an attempt to get something—*anything*—under control. Having life turned upside-down is a very disconcerting feeling; having anything under control helps—even if it's only making sure that the plants don't need watering.

5. Respect the person's unique loss. Probably the most difficult thing is that every journey of loss is different. What comforted one person may or may not comfort someone else . . . even if the loss looks the same from the outside. One of the kindest things

that anyone said to me was a statement made by a woman whose husband died exactly the same way mine did—from a brain aneurysm. That woman was Gladys Andersen—my brother-in-law's mom. The difference in our stories was that Clifford and Gladys had been married for 56 years, while Scott and I had been married for 27. Though the circumstances looked identical, Gladys wrote in a card, "I have no idea how this would have felt . . . and it has grieved me for you that you only got to have him for 27 years." In my heart, I have thanked Gladys many times for that comment. She didn't just "lump me in" with everyone else who had lost a spouse. She acknowledged it specifically: Rebecca, Scott, 27 years. Her comments validated my loss as one of a kind. She respected *my* loss.

And so, dear comforter . . . may the Lord bless you as you seek to comfort your friend or family member. May He pour out upon you the wisdom of the Comforter. May He give you the grace to know when to speak and when to be silent. May He give you hands to help, memories to share, and endurance in the process. In the name of Jesus, Amen.

Part 2

SURVIVAL: LIVING IN EMOTIONAL INTENSIVE CARE

HOW DO I VIEW GOD?

Choices: How Do I View God?

In high school I had an English teacher who had a very soured picture of God. I have no idea what loss or disappointment may have brought him to this viewpoint, but one day in class, he described God as completely arbitrary: "We are like ants, and some days God throws us some grains of sugar, and other days He decides to stomp on us."

I obviously don't agree with that viewpoint, but in the middle of loss and grief, it's easy to feel like God is suddenly against you. (See p. 95.) To add to the problem, many believers have the idea that if you're "good," then everything will go well for you, and if you're "bad"—well—it won't. Some people call this "two ways theology." You don't have to live very long, however, to discover that life isn't usually quite that easy to define! Even so, there are verses that seem to indicate that this "two ways" idea is correct. Read all of Deuteronomy 28 to see the blessings on obedience and curses on disobedience. On the other hand, Jeremiah laments that the wicked prosper (see Jer. 12:1; see also Job 12:6; Hab. 1:4; Eccles. 8:14).

How do we put this all together to understand what God is really like?

Personally, I've come to look at these verses as "big picture" (the long-term impact of obedience) in contrast to "small picture" (the short-term impact of suffering).

When all is said and done, I will be blessed because I have followed the Lord (*big picture*). That doesn't mean there won't be bumps along the way (*small picture*). The bumps we encounter generally have to do with the fact that we live in a world that has been broken by sin, and the fallout of sin is death, disease, disaster, broken relationships, hard work, thorns in the field, labor in delivery, and, worst of all, separation from God. (Thank you, Adam and Eve, for being disobedient to your one rule! Truth be told, however, if they hadn't done it, I probably would have. Or you would've. We're all susceptible to thinking that our plan is better than God's.)

There are a lot of metaphors we can use to support this "big picture and small picture" concept. If the farmer doesn't plow, he won't reap a harvest. If I don't exercise and work my muscles, they won't be there when I need them. If a tree doesn't experience the stress of wind and drought, its roots won't go deep. In the same way, the challenges of life help us to grow. I don't believe God "does" bad things to us, like my English teacher suggested. Bad things happen because the world is broken; it is God who steps in to redeem our brokenness and put things back together.

Big picture; small picture.

So what is God really like? In Exodus 34:6-7, He offers us a description of Himself:

> The LORD, the LORD God, merciful and gracious, long-suffering, and abounding in goodness and truth, keeping mercy for thousands, forgiving iniquity and

transgression and sin, by no means clearing the guilty, visiting the iniquity of the fathers upon the children and the children's children to the third and the fourth generation.

Before we look at the five terms God uses to describe Himself, we're going to look at the second half of the verse, because that's the part we tend to get nervous about. Essentially, it means that the Lord forgives all who repent, and He judges those who do not repent. If you have repented for your sin, forgiveness is yours. The debt is clear. The rest of the verse can look like maybe God is vindictive, but all this is really saying is that sin begets sin. Anyone who turns to God with a repentant heart *will* be forgiven. "If we confess our sins, He is faithful and just to forgive us our sins and to cleanse us from all unrighteousness" (1 John 1:9).

Now, let's look at the five words God uses to describe Himself. Our tendency is to zoom over them, but let's take a closer look, because these traits of God have the ability and promise to greatly impact our journey.

The first word is "merciful." This means that His heart toward us is compassionate, but because the Hebrew word is used only of the Lord, it implies a kind of compassion that is above and beyond anything humans can offer.

"Gracious" carries the idea of "stooping in kindness to an inferior." Think of that! God will always meet us where we are. Can I say that again? *Always.*

When we talk about "longsuffering," we typically define it as "patience." On a grief journey, that is an important trait—He is patient with our process, and He knows what we can handle. "He knows our frame . . . that we are dust" (Ps. 103:14).

"Goodness" is a difficult word to define in this context, because the concept has more to do with God's covenant love toward us than with "being nice," which is how we tend to use it in English. In other words, when we talk about God's goodness, we are talking about the fact that He has made a covenant with us, and He will never give up on us or leave us. "Covenant" does not always mean much in our culture, but in God's kingdom, covenant is permanent.

Finally, God uses the word "truth"—which literally means stability, trustworthiness and faithfulness—to describe Himself. He is a safe place to build.

Merciful. Gracious. Longsuffering. Goodness. Truth.

There is nothing to fear in our God. He is on this journey with us for the long haul. He will never leave us or forsake us (see Heb. 13:5), and His heart toward us is always goodness, mercy and truth. He is a safe, stable place where we can rest when the losses of life overtake us.

Big picture; small picture.

The loss I faced was a death. The loss you face may be something else entirely, but every loss comes back to the fact that the world got broken. We may interpret "two-ways theology" as being too cut-and-dried. But there *are* two ways to live: God's way or our way. Our way may sound easy—even good—in the small picture, but it produces ruin in the big picture. God's way may look harder as we make our day-to-day choices. But in the big picture it leads to life everlasting!

May I invite you to walk the Lord's path even though right now it may look cold and dark? In the big picture, it still leads to life. It still leads to a future and a hope. It still leads to blessing. Proverbs 12:28 says, "In the way of righteousness is life, and in its pathway there is no death."

Wrestling: What Does the Bible Say About Loss?

The Bible says that we are not to "sorrow as [those] who have no hope" (1 Thess. 4:13), and Christians are quick to quote that verse in the face of grief and loss. But I have found that people tend to use this verse to imply that we are not to sorrow. At all. Period. We read it almost as: *If* you sorrow, then you have no hope.

This idea is evidenced in some of the things people have said to me about their own losses:

- "Thank you for giving me permission to cry."
- "I cry all the time . . . I wish I had more faith."
- "Just focus on Jesus."
- "I feel guilty because I didn't have enough faith to keep my husband alive."

These kinds of statements indicate a lack of understanding both of Paul's intent and of how God created us. Paul isn't asking us to deny grief; he is showing us *how* to process it: "Yes . . . we sorrow. But don't sorrow like those without the hope of a future—here or in eternity. Don't sorrow like those without Christ." After all, our hope *is Jesus!* (See 1 Thess. 1:3; 1 Tim. 1:1; Titus 2:13; 1 Pet. 1:13.)

In the ancient Roman world, "sorrowing without hope" would have involved sacrifices to idols, forms of ancestor worship, and appeasement of evil spirits. In certain quarters it may have even involved cutting. *That* is sorrowing without hope. Sorrowing that way would, of course, be completely different than sorrowing *with* hope—with the hope of Christ, with the hope of heaven, and with the hope of Jesus' return.

The statements above also merit a second look, because they betray some misunderstandings that we are all prone to. Let's weigh them against what Scripture tells us.

"Thank you for giving me permission to cry."

This statement was made to me by a widow whose husband had died several years before . . . and she had denied herself the release of tears because she believed that to do so would be "sorrowing like the world." This decision was made in a sincere desire to live a life honoring to God. But consider these verses:

- Job cries out, "My eyes pour out tears to God" (Job 16:20). Weeping tears in front of Jesus is the *only* safe place to cry them.
- David asks the Lord to "put my tears into Your bottle" (Ps. 56:8). *Put these tears in safe-keeping, Lord! Value, comfort and heal the pain that I have experienced.*
- Isaiah writes, "He will swallow up death forever, and the Lord GOD will wipe away tears from all faces" (Isa. 25:8). This isn't a rebuke for weeping; it's a promise of comfort! Though Jesus has conquered death and the sting has been taken away (see 1 Cor. 15:55-57), we still live with the consequences of our broken world until He comes again. *May that day come soon!*

"I cry all the time . . . I wish I had more faith."

The woman who said this had suffered the loss of five family members within 24 months. She did cry all the time . . . and with good reason. The fact is, crying doesn't have anything to do with faith. Weeping and sadness have to do with emotion; faith is a choice based on what we believe. Despite death, despite loss, despite grief, despite tears . . . I *choose to believe* that the Lord will walk me through the Valley, and that He will sustain me on the journey. Tears are not an indication of lack of faith.

"Just focus on Jesus."

Not long after Scott's death, a couple offered this exhortation to me as a way to get through my first holidays without my husband. I *did* understand what they meant. But I have to admit that, over time, I became very wary of the "easy answers." *Just do this and it will all be fine.*

That Christmas was truly horrible—we all missed Scott. We missed his presence at the dinner table; we missed giving him gifts; we missed his terrible gift-wrapping skills. To make matters worse, the holiday was compounded by rain, two kids with the flu, and an emergency appendectomy. We barbecued in the rain to prepare a meal hardly anyone could eat. And yet . . . in the midst of it all . . . we were so thankful. Thankful that Jesus had been born! Thankful that He was already showing Himself faithful to us on this journey! Thankful that we were all together!

The two extremes of experience—dealing with a loss *and* living in thanksgiving for the fact that Jesus came—really can go hand in hand, but to deny one in the place of the other simply seemed like a diversionary tactic.

"I feel guilty because I didn't have enough faith to keep my husband alive."

I wept over this email from a widow. The guilt she felt, layered upon the grief she was living in, was horrific.

And unnecessary.

Our faith is not what keeps people alive, because it is never *our* works that accomplish anything. We're called to pray and believe; the rest is Jesus' job. Sometimes He heals the person we're praying for. But sometimes it is simply that person's appointment. "The days in their book" are finished (see Ps. 139:16).

We grieve when people we love die. But we must never forget Paul's words: "To live is Christ, and to die is gain" (Phil. 1:21). *Gain?* For our loved one, yes. While we grieve, we must always remember that *heaven is never a loss*.

Here, we have considered only 1 Thessalonians 4:13, and while we will be looking at other passages together later, can I encourage you to do a little of your own study as well? Scripture has quite a lot to say about grief:

- There is a whole book of the Bible called "Lamentations"—funeral dirges. The prophet Jeremiah was lamenting—grieving, sorrowing over—the loss of a nation, the loss of a city, the loss of God's people.
- Read through the psalms. David's honesty with God about His painful emotions—bewailing his misery, reflecting on his sorrows, pouring out his tears—is always a comfort to me. If he can be that honest, then so can I. Jesus knows, and He understands, because He Himself has been "acquainted with grief" (Isa. 53:3; see also John 11:35).

• The book of Job provides an up-close look at someone who is wrestling his way through his own journey of loss—and asking all the hard questions.

Lesson: We Have a Choice

The idea of having choices goes against how many of us view the Lord. Of course we know that salvation is a choice—it is the most important choice we will ever make. But after that, we view our life in God as almost robotic. "He has it all mapped out, and all we do is walk along the road He lays down before us." We define things in terms of God's "perfect will" (*when we're doing things right*) and His "permissive will" (*when we get off the path and He helps us anyway*).

Until my journey through the Valley, I don't think I ever really thought about the fact that the Lord offers us a much more intentional and interactive life than that. Of course, we are supposed to do what God wants us to, and what His Word teaches. The fact is, however, that *every* time we choose to do God's will, we are engaging our will, too. We are actively involved in the process, not passively sitting in a chair waiting for some kind of heavenly download.

It's a choice.

What I learned on my journey was how to choose life in the middle of loss and grief and death. It would've been so easy to wallow in self-pity. And—yes—life was dark for a very long time. It isn't called the Valley of the Shadow for nothing. In that darkness, I learned to cling to God; I learned to hold His hand. Though this is not the "first choice" presented in this book, it *was* the first choice I made on my journey: Whose hand was I going to hold?

Jesus picked up my hand the day my husband died.

That morning, I woke early. Really early. I knew what I was facing that day. I knew that unless God did a miracle, this was going to be Scott's last day. When I woke at 4 AM, I knew that I wasn't going back to sleep—so I got dressed and went to the hospital.

Members of our pastoral staff had sat with Scott all night long—a kindness that I did not underestimate then or now. It was important to me that *Scott was never alone.* They very kindly stayed with him all night so that my children and I could sleep and be ready for whatever the next day held.

Now, arriving at the hospital, I wanted one last chance to hold my husband's hand—one last chance to talk to him here on this earth (though he was unconscious and incapable of responding).

What do you do in that moment?

I sat down, took Scott's hand, and leaned my head on the bed-rail. *"Jesus,"* I whispered, *"I don't know what to do here except to cling to You."* Immediately His voice whispered back into my heart:

"All other ground is sinking sand. Even Scott."

Of course, I knew the song:

> *My hope is built on nothing less*
> *Than Jesus' blood and righteousness . . .*
> *On Christ the solid rock I stand*
> *All other ground is sinking sand.*[1]

And I knew the verse:

Therefore whoever hears these sayings of Mine, and does them, I will liken him to a wise man who built his house on the rock (Matt. 7:24).

And I knew where to run:

> *That Rock is Christ (see 1 Cor. 10:4).*

In the first moments of my journey, God presented me with my first choice. I understood that I was going to have to let go of Scott's hand. I also knew that I wasn't strong enough to not hold *someone's* hand—and I determined that Jesus' hand was the one I would hold.

In the face of loss, many "hands" will be offered.

There is the "hand" that blames God and rebels against Him, choosing to live in anger. It's tempting, in the middle of life's losses, to reject God's hand and stand with our backs to Him—as if our refusal to look Him in the face will make the journey easier or will punish Him for the fact that something is broken in our lives. Believe me—something is *always* broken in us! The fact is that Jesus is the only One who can bring wholeness.

There is the "hand" that offers the counterfeit of human comfort. In our pain, we can be tempted to graspingly reach for anyone, anytime, anyplace. We want the comfort, fellowship and strength of others, but reaching for that hand in a bar . . . or online . . . or wherever else . . . only comforts for a moment. Recognize your vulnerability on this road and have people to whom you are accountable. (See p. 149.)

Then there is the "hand" that seeks to create a shrine. This hand actually keeps us clinging to the past—a past that no longer exists. As hard as it is to admit that something is over, living in the past will ultimately keep us drowning in grief.

All loss requires making this choice. Ultimately, it isn't the choice of holding a person's hand or holding God's hand; it is the choice of holding God's hand or trying to walk this journey in our own strength.

Moses experienced a moment like this, when he had to choose which hand he would hold to go forward. On the heels of the Israelites' reverting to idol worship, Moses received the command from the Lord to leave Sinai and lead the people toward the Promised Land. He faced a real dilemma here. He had clearly seen that he had a rather unruly group of people to lead! And now he was supposed to lead them into God's promise? On the heels of disobedience, idolatry and plague, Moses was supposed to focus on the future. In that moment, he said some very poignant words to the Lord:

> If Your Presence does not go with us, do not bring us up from here (Exod. 33:15).

Moses decided whose hand he was going to hold. He had a hard journey ahead. So did I. So do you. But resting firmly on the solid rock and holding Jesus' hand will get you safely to the future.

Application: Taking Stock of Stress

If you're anything like I was at the beginning of my journey, your stress level is really high. In those initial weeks and months, I found myself eating a lot of macaroni and cheese—not because

it was my favorite food, but because my stomach was in such turmoil, it was the only thing I could keep down. My evenings were
spent watching old movies—not because that was my favorite
activity, but because the evenings were so long and lonely, that
was the only thing that kept my thoughts diverted. These were
obvious signs that my stress level had reached an all-time high!

I didn't realize, however, the kind of physical toll that grief
(and its accompanying stress) can take on a person until about
five years later, when I was getting sick all the time. Colds.
Allergies. Sinus infections. The flu. It just went on and on. I had
always been the kind of person who never got sick, but now I was
downing antibiotics multiple times a year. I've since dealt with
all of this, but I wish I had known up front some of the things I
learned the hard way. Here's what I wish I had been made aware
of sooner:

1. *Go to the doctor.* I went to the doctor "by accident."
   I already had a check-up scheduled and just kept the
   appointment. I'm thankful that I did. First, because
   Scott and I had the same primary-care doctor, he
   was able to look at all of Scott's records and answer
   a lot of questions that I still had. Second, he alerted
   me to depression danger signs to watch for. While
   I didn't wind up facing an unhealthy depression
   level, I did let the people closest to me know what
   to look out for. Their observation served as a safety
   net for me. Third, it gave me an idea of how I was
   doing physically.

2. *The stress test.* In the mid-1960s, two psychiatrists con-
   ducted a study to evaluate how stress levels could be

an indicator of susceptibility to illness. Did higher stress levels make people more vulnerable to health problems? I wish I had found this information sooner, and I encourage you to search the Web for the Holmes-Rahe Stress Inventory and take it for yourself. It will help you evaluate your stress level.

3. *Diet and exercise.* I already told you about my macaroni and cheese extravaganza. Thankfully that was only for a season. As things settled down (a little), I started trying to get a bit more exercise and eat more normally. Looking back, I don't think I did as well as I should have, and I would encourage you to learn from my mistakes to take your vitamins and eat your vegetables—even if you have to do it by having a vegetable juice drink or using the "greens" powder mix from the health food store.

4. *Evaluating emotional pain:* I recognized from the beginning that the emotional pain and grief I was in was not the worst pain someone could experience. Scott and I had a happy marriage, and though he died and I missed him terribly, there was no love that was lost or trust that had been broken. I was still provided for (via life insurance) by a husband who loved me. Sad though this was, it wasn't the worst thing. However, I've walked the journey of divorce with friends who suddenly have a former husband who is re-writing their history: *"I never loved you."* Or who refuses to provide for them. Or who won't support the children. It was during this season that I came across the phrases "clean pain" and "dirty

pain." What I had experienced was clean pain—a clean wound. Bandage it up and let it heal. But others who have experienced dirty pain have some different issues to process. Being aware of the difference will be important in determining the kind of help you should seek. Which leads me to the next point . . .

5. *Get counseling.* There are professionals who are equipped to help us walk this road, and there is no shame in seeing a counselor. Again, needs differ. I went to see a counselor three or four times in the first several years. You may need more, or you may not feel a need to use this resource at all. For me, I primarily needed to know that I was processing everything I should be, that I was "normal" in my process, and that I wasn't getting stuck anywhere along the way. I would recommend, as a starting place, seeing if your church offers any type of pastoral counseling or grief classes.

6. *Identifying the areas where you need help.* Not everyone needs the same types of help in getting life back on track. I chuckled to myself several times when people kept sending me food. Not that I didn't appreciate it—I was thankful for it! (Especially the macaroni and cheese.) But I realized that the Church in general defaults to an Acts 6 model when faced with a death crisis—feed the widows! My bigger needs had to do with figuring out the areas that Scott usually took care of: finances, yard and car. One of the initial steps in this process is simply to determine what you do and do not need help with.

7. *I did something nice for myself every day*—something that was stress relieving. This is a very individual decision. Stress relief can be anything from tennis to a bubble bath to an old movie to dinner with a friend. Give yourself space when you need to. Something helpful that I read in this season was this: "Give yourself permission to be in emotional intensive care." So often, we think we need to just "stay strong." There are plenty of things you will need to be strong for, so take time to nurture yourself a bit. Do something nice for yourself every day.

Interaction: Photo Album

Photographs had never meant more to me than they did in this season. I had pictures of Scott everywhere! But walking through my house one day, I looked at a picture of him and said out loud, "Your expression never changes anymore!"

Of course it didn't. It was a photograph. This is what I had left. He was gone.

Initially, the moment shocked me with the realization of "how over" everything really was; the relationship we had was not going to change or grow anymore. Scott was not going to grow any older. (I have to admit that 10 years down the road, he is looking younger and younger!)

That moment also brought me to a day of going through the family pictures. Though his expression did not change in any one picture, I had a record of his many different expressions in a lifetime of photographs. That day I created a photo album that I still get out once in a while. I have all of those pictures on my iPad, too.

I chose pictures that showed interests and expressions—serious and fun, young and old. I chose pictures that showed his humor, pictures of places we had visited, pictures of him with each of our children. I found the one picture that includes us with all of our children and their spouses. It was taken just a few months before Scott died, but it's the only one that includes my son-in-law, James, because he and Lindsey had just begun to date. Precious, precious picture. The only one with all eight of us.

I included pictures of Scott . . .

. . . at Christmas events at our church.

. . . with a fish he caught in Alaska.

. . . throwing out the first pitch at Dodger Stadium.

. . . at our wedding.

. . . at the Grand Canyon.

. . . dancing with Lindsey at our niece's wedding.

. . . with Kyle in Israel.

. . . with Brian in Washington, D.C.

. . . squidging his nose up on one side the way he did.

I found them all! Going through the photos made me laugh and it made me cry. Remembering was joyous that day! It provided me with a great idea for Scott's parents for Mother's Day and Father's Day one year. The photo album gave me a way to see all of the joy of our family, and best of all . . . it showed his expressions.

Note

1. "The Solid Rock," lyrics by Edward Mote, music by William B. Bradbury.

WHERE WILL I BUILD?

Choices: Where Will I Build?

During the first months of my journey, I spent a lot of time walking and thinking . . . and walking and thinking. This was a complete readjustment of life at every dimension. There was so much coming at me, and whenever I got the chance to just think—to mentally "make this real"—that's what I did.

One day as I was walking and thinking, and asking the Lord for direction and definition, He impressed upon my heart the following words:

> For quite a while, you are going to be living in two worlds: the world you feel and the world you believe. You have to process both of them . . . *but you get to pick which one you're going to build in.*

Think about that for a moment: *Process both . . . build in one.*

This was a radical shift for me! So often in my life, people around me had presented the emotional aspects of life as suspect. Untrustworthy. Maybe even *unworthy* for a believer to spend time and energy on. I don't think I fully believed that, because my parents did a brilliant job balancing the "human" and "holy" parts of life. Still, when you hear something often enough, it starts to seep into your thinking.

I understood what the Lord was saying, and I knew where to build! I'd seen people build where they feel, and I knew I didn't want to go down that path. Emotions are a bad foundation on which to build your future, because they can change every day. When you're building, you want to build on something . . . *changeless*. Our beliefs are where we are to build our lives.

That agreed upon, however, let's look for a moment at emotions and how Christians tend to view them, because if we're supposed to process "the world we feel," we need to have a clear picture of what we even think about our feelings.

My experience has taught me that a lot of Christians tend to be nervous about emotions. The verse I've usually heard used to caution against listening to your emotions is Jeremiah 17:9: "The heart is deceitful above all things, and desperately wicked; who can know it?"

Well . . . Jesus can know it. First Samuel 16:7 says that God "looks at the heart." He is perfectly capable of knowing my heart, discerning what's good and bad in it, and helping me to see those things, too. Not every emotion in my heart is wicked. My love for my family isn't deceitful. My love for the Lord isn't deceitful. While I agree that emotions *can* be deceitful, the fact that they are present doesn't mean they are necessarily untrue or lying to us.

When we talk about grief and loss and the emotion that accompanies that process, I have found it helpful to look deeper and figure out where the emotion is coming from. For example, my grief over Scott's death was, of course, flowing out of my love for him and the fact that I missed him. But several years later, when life started to be "good again" (see p. 179), I went around for a while feeling bad. Looking deeper, I discovered that I actually felt guilty about being happy with my life when Scott was no longer in it. That was a deceitful emotion, because it was leading me away from where the Lord wanted to take me. Frankly, it was leading me away from where Scott would want me to go, too.

Processing emotions requires us to look a little deeper into our hearts. This is why we should never process emotion apart from the Lord. He is the only one who can see the heart.

> For the LORD does not see as man sees; for man looks at the outward appearance, but the LORD looks at the heart (1 Sam. 16:7).

> For the LORD searches all hearts and understands all the intent of the thoughts (1 Chron. 28:9).

> Search me, O God, and know my heart; try me, and know my anxieties (Ps. 139:23).

So what do you believe? And where are you going to build?

To answer those questions, let's look at the first building God asked people to build, and the first thing He asked them to believe.

The first building the Lord asked people to build was the Tabernacle in the wilderness. We often think of the Tabernacle as merely a place to bring sacrifices, but its purpose was so that God could dwell among His people (see Exod. 25:8). To miss that fact is to miss a picture of the heart of God that longs to be close to us. The purpose of the building and the worship that took place there was to invite His presence. Psalm 22:3 hints at this same idea: "You are . . . enthroned in the praises of Israel." It is significant to note that the word translated as "enthroned" literally means "to dwell, to remain, to abide." God wants to dwell with us! He is so committed to this that He eventually sent Jesus, who is also called Immanuel—*God with us* (see Isa. 7:14; Matt. 1:23). It is our worship that invites Him into our midst. Into our homes. Into our hearts. Into our journeys.

The first thing the Lord asked people to believe was His Word. He gave one instruction to Adam and Eve, and it is the *only* thing the snake attacked. "Did God *really* say . . . ?" (see Gen. 3:1). The devil questioned God's goodness toward Adam and Eve in withholding one thing. Then, by questioning God's Word, he brought them to a place of compromise.

God calls us to trust and believe His Word. When we're tempted to doubt, or to fear—He calls us to believe Him. That sounds easy, but when it comes to living it out in the middle of your soul's darkest night, it gets a lot harder.

And it doesn't happen by accident.

On my journey, I did deal with both worlds. The walk-through-able part of the journey was incredibly difficult. And long. In the world of my emotions, I have cried a lot of tears and said a lot of hurt, angry and fearful words to God. (He's a big God and He can take my outbursts. I don't intend to sound trite; He really does know that we are just made of dust [see Ps. 103:14].)

When it came to building, I chose to believe . . . *Him*. And His Word. I chose to keep worshiping and inviting His presence and His rulership into my life. When the journey was done and I walked out of the dark tunnel of grief, I realized that the choice to rebuild had actually been made at the beginning of the journey. The moment I decided to "build where I believe," I began building my future.

Wrestling: Living in the Cocoon

One of the ways that I described my life to myself early on was to say that I was in a cocoon: I was in a very dark place, and I knew that eventually the Lord would bring me out of it. But I did not like the cocoon. Not at all. It was dark. It was small. It was uncomfortable. I knew there would come a day when I got to emerge as a butterfly, but that moment was far in the future. For the time being, I was in a cocoon: *Dark. Constricted. Hot.*

One day, tired of the "constrictedness" that the cocoon brought, I Googled "What happens in the cocoon?" Now, if you loved science in school, you may already know the answer to that question; but it was news to me. All I remembered was that in my science book, there were three pictures: The first one showed a caterpillar crawling along a branch. The second one showed a cocoon hanging from the branch. The third one showed a butterfly flying off into the sunset. Clearly something was missing in my understanding of this process. Hence Google.

What I learned amazed me—and sent me to the Word! I discovered that what was happening in the dark of the cocoon was that the caterpillar was dissolving into liquid. (Yuck!) Then, gradually, it would reform into *a completely new creature*, but with the same DNA. The caterpillar-soup-stage is pretty bad; but if we submit to the process of what God wants to do in us, it will ultimately be beautiful beyond anything we could've ever dreamed or imagined (see Eph. 3:20).

As much as I was living in impatience over my process, I had to admit, this was pretty amazing information. Think of it: *a completely new creature!* Wow! I had read something like that before, too—which is what sent me to the Word.

We know this caterpillar-to-butterfly process to be called "metamorphosis," and that word—or at least a form of it—is actually used four times in the New Testament. In Romans 12:2, the apostle Paul calls all believers in Jesus Christ to be *transformed*—in Greek, *metamorphousthe*—and not be fashioned after this world:

> Do not be conformed to this world, but be transformed
> by the renewing of your mind, that you may prove what
> is that good and acceptable and perfect will of God
> (Rom. 12:2).

The same word is used when Jesus is transfigured (see Matt. 17:2; Mark. 9:2); He was transformed—made into something new. Even Jesus *metamorphousthe*! And the same thing is promised to us: "if anyone is in Christ, he is a new creation; old things have passed away; behold, all things have become new" (2 Cor. 5:17). Finally:

> But we all, with unveiled face, beholding as in a mirror
> the glory of the Lord, are being transformed [*metamor-
> phoumetha*] into the same image from glory to glory, just
> as by the Spirit of the Lord (2 Cor. 3:18).

As I meditated on the idea of being in a cocoon, and what takes place there, I was struck by a similar phrase that appears in several Scripture verses: "in the shadow of His wing" (see Pss. 17:8; 57:1; 63:7):

In the shadow of Your wings I will make my refuge,
until these calamities have passed by (Ps. 57:1).

This verse described exactly where I was: in calamity, in need of a refuge. What made it similar to the cocoon was the darkness. But unlike the cocoon, this felt:

Safe. Warm. Embraced.

I learned a few things about darkness, too. I learned that there is *my* darkness and *His* darkness. My darkness leads to confusion, but His darkness obscures things for my benefit. Sometimes it's good for us not to see everything—not to know everything. Like a wise parent, the Lord waits until "the child" is ready to know certain information. God met Moses in darkness: "Moses drew near the thick darkness where God was" (Exod. 20:21; see also 2 Sam. 22:12; 1 Kings 8:12; Ps. 18:11).

Scripture also tells us that He will bring light to our darkness (see Ps. 18:28; Isa. 42:16; Luke 1:79). Most moving to me was the darkness that surrounded Jesus on *His* day of darkness—His crucifixion (see Matt. 27:45; Mark. 15:33). Isaiah writes that God gives "treasures [out] of darkness" (Isa. 45:3), and on that spectacular, dreadful day, God gave us the greatest treasure when He "delivered us from the power of darkness and conveyed us into the kingdom of the Son of His love" (Col. 1:13).

I walked a spectacular, dreadful journey, too. These pictures from Scripture reminded me that though I was in a dark place, the Lord was still at work. Though I was currently living in a constricted place, the "butterfly" days were ahead. I could count on it, because He was committed to transforming me and making all things new.

During this season—that still seemed very dark—I was sitting in my backyard one day and a butterfly fluttered into the yard. I watched as it flew to the far end of my swimming pool, went up really high, and then swooped down over the water to the other end of the pool. I figured that the heat of the air must have changed along with the water depth, creating a nice "swoop." Looked kind of fun! But what really struck me was that this butterfly then went back to the far end of the pool and repeated the whole process. Again. And again. And again! It must've been kind of like a butterfly roller coaster. I had to laugh to myself because . . . this butterfly was playing. It was out of the cocoon and playing!

One day, about two and a half years into my journey, I realized that the Lord *really had* made everything new. I lived in a new place. I had a new job. Our family was beginning a new generation. I had unwittingly begun to decorate my home with colors I had never used before. I had new friends, new clothes, new travels and new experiences. I learned to swim, developed a love for bracelets, and even started liking foods that I had never liked before! (Just hand over the sushi and no one will get hurt.) I also had new vision for my future. Jesus was indeed—and still is—transforming my life and making all things new. I think it's called metamorphosis . . .

Sort of like coming out of a cocoon.

Lesson: Dealing with Depression

Grief hurts. Depression hurts. I would be remiss not to acknowledge those two facts. During the course of a journey through the Valley of the Shadow, depression can creep up on us—and before we know it, we're in a dangerous place.

That is nothing to mess around with.

I have seen people in all ranges of this, from those who experience "feelings of depression that last for an afternoon" to those who are suffering from ongoing debilitating depression and are in need of medical help. This is nothing to be afraid of, but in order to face this challenge of the journey, we need to be honest about what we're going through, and be willing to take some specific steps.

See your doctor. I recommend that you see your doctor early in your journey (see page 49). Let him or her know what has been happening in your life, and ask about the warning signs of depression that you—and those around you—should watch for. Keeping your doctor informed about all parts of your life will help him or her advise you as you progress through your journey. He or she will know of many resources that may be of help to you, including any support groups or classes offered through his or her medical practice or your local hospital.

If your doctor recommends medication, please know that there is no shame in taking it. The Bible says that "every good gift . . . comes down from the Father" (Jas. 1:17). If a medication helps people, I would call that a "good gift." I would call medical professionals "good gifts" as well.

I can appreciate your concern if the idea of medication makes you nervous. I once suggested to a widower that he go to see his doctor. (Seriously . . . that's *all* I said.) His immediate response was, "I'm not taking any medication." I hadn't said anything about that, but clearly this was an area of apprehension for him. So if this is a concern for you, too, please know that you have the right to ask your doctor all of the questions that concern you:

- How long would I have to take this?
- How long do I take this before I notice an improvement?
- Are there any side effects?
- What are the steps for going off of this medication later?
- Is it addictive?

Ask everything.

You also have the right to choose whether to go down that road or not. But I would suggest that you make that decision with the input of those closest to you, as well as in consultation with medical professionals who know you and your history. In fact, it would be good to take someone with you to your doctor's appointment. *Involve trustworthy friends.* Give those closest to you the information from the doctor *and* give them permission to check up on you. At this stage of the journey, it can be tricky to maintain a balance between needing to have a little isolation (emotional intensive care) and involving people in your life. You need both, so give those you trust permission to challenge you if they see something that indicates that perhaps you should visit your doctor again. As an RN friend of mine says, "When in doubt, check it out." If you are concerned about any depression you are facing—go to the doctor.

For me, I just sometimes needed to be around people. On my journey, there were a couple of times when I just knew I should not go home after work and sit in an empty house. I *just knew* that I was vulnerable that day. My strategy for that was to postpone going home for a few hours, and to spend that time around people—whether that meant hanging out at my sister's house, or going to church, or strolling the mall. In those moments, that generally took care of it.

The need for laughter. This journey can be so hard that sometimes we need to be intentional about seeking out humor. At least I did. I remember thinking one day that if I didn't find something to laugh about, I was going to cry myself to death. That was, frankly, not a pleasant day; however, it did point out to me that I needed to be intentional about adding some laughter to my life. The Bible says that "a merry heart does good, like a medicine" (Prov. 17:22). I needed that medicine! So one of the things I did was to develop a humor library. Movies, cartoon books, sometimes the photo album of Scott (see p. 52)—things that simply made me laugh. I needed those splashes of fun throughout the week.

Application: Building the Foundation

Living in an earthquake-prone area, I've learned the importance of a foundation. One thing that's interesting about foundations in our area is that most of them are slabs of concrete. There are few basements. After all, do you *really* want a basement when the house above you could start shaking at any moment? My husband, who grew up on the East Coast, thought that not having a basement was really strange—until his first earthquake. "I get it now," he admitted.

So our foundations are slabs. At one point in the '80s, new earthquake preparedness criteria came out, one of which involved making sure your house was actually *attached* to the foundation, and not just sitting on top of it! (I know . . . crazy Californians!)

I think this is an apt metaphor for dealing with crisis and loss: What is your foundation? And, are you attached to it? If you are, though things may still sway when the world is shaking, you won't come loose from your solid foundation.

Jesus talked about foundations in Matthew 7. He talked about people who built on the sand versus those who built on solid rock. Building on sand is quick and easy. And, hey—it's beachfront property! But the sands quickly slip away in the first storm, and so does the house.

Building on the rock takes a lot longer, and it requires more work. It probably costs more, too. You dig down to bedrock. You pour the foundation. *Then* you get to start building! That's a lot of process before you even start the house! But the house is solid. It will weather the storm. Maybe the "house" you've been living in is getting you through this crisis just fine. But chances are that if you are building toward a life that looks different, you will need to re-establish a foundation and build a new house. Just make sure it's "on the rock."

Scripture tells us that Jesus is the Rock (see 1 Cor. 3:11; 10:4; Isa. 28:16). He is the only safe, solid place to build a future. While this obviously has to do with salvation, the concept can be applied in many areas of life, of moving forward, and of building a future. This isn't the time for shortcuts. Building on sand may be fast and easy, but it won't hold up for the long haul.

As you begin to look at things you need to process in order to build a solid future, this is not a time to look for the easy way. In this part of the process, it's tempting to let things go; but every time we do that, we are subtly declaring that we don't think we have a good future. For example, for a period of many months, I basically stopped cooking. I was tired after work, and I would pick up convenience food on my way home. (I know—not much better than macaroni and cheese!) There came a day when I realized that if I was really going to build a future, I needed to address this simple area of my life. I was so out of practice by then that I actually forgot the sugar when I made a batch of gingerbread! (I re-named the recipe "Cinnamon-Salt Surprise.") All this is to say, when you're building a future—everything counts. Here are a few other areas to consider:

- If you need new skills for work, don't opt for the weekend seminar certification that may be fast, but ultimately isn't marketable. Find out what you need to do to prepare for the career you want, and make the investment in schooling. Build on the rock.
- Look realistically at what is going to work for your family. How old are your kids? What do they need? How are you going to make sure those needs are met? Just as you don't want to come out of this journey with unnecessary baggage, so too you don't want your kids to, either.
- Reevaluate the extra-curricular activities of your life. Do you volunteer anywhere? At the kids' school? At church? This may be a time to step back and get your foundation in order so that you can go back to your activities long-term, with energy and enthusiasm, rather than forcing yourself to do everything that "looks normal" and burning yourself out. Do the

things that solidly build the foundation in every part of your life.

- What does your home look like? Is it being cared for? Or does it look like you've given up? All of these things contribute to the foundation. Setting the things in place that work in a new season takes time. If this doesn't happen by next Thursday at 9 AM, don't beat yourself up over it. Reevaluate what you're doing and reset some goals. I have a list that I call "The Perfect Day." If the perfect day ever arrived, this is what I think it would look like . . . and it would happen every day![1] I probably hit it about once every two weeks; but it's certainly better than never hitting it at all. Maybe someday I'll move up to once a week!

- How about you? Are you taking care of yourself? I'm not just talking about medically either. Not to get too personal, but have you opted for the "all baggy" wardrobe? Or are you going for the do-it-yourself haircut? Been there, done both of those! While I understand those things, they subtly send us a message that life is over. Re-investing in caring for ourselves can also help us to keep moving ahead, affirming over and over: *I do have a future!* Keep aiming at the future in everything, from the largest things to the smallest things.

Making the necessary investments of time and energy is not easy. There were moments when I wanted to huddle into a fetal position and let the world pass me by. You'll have those moments, too. But keep building; keep preparing; keep working on the foundation.

Then, of course, there's the question of staying attached to *the* foundation: Jesus. If you've never found that safe, solid place in Jesus Christ, you can accept Him into your life this very moment. The Bible says that "if you confess with your mouth the Lord Jesus and believe in your heart that God has raised Him from the dead, you *will* be saved" (Rom. 10:9, emphasis added). If you "believe in your heart," you can pray right now:

> *Dear Jesus Christ,*
>   *I believe that You are the Savior of the world who died for my sins, and I accept You into my life right now. Forgive me. Make my life new. For this journey that I'm on, I take Your hand and ask that You walk with me through it.*
>   *I ask this in Your name, amen.*

Now, "confess with your mouth"—say it out loud to someone. My guess is that if you are holding this book, someone who knows the Lord gave it to you. Call them. Tell them about your decision. They will be able to help you walk forward in this new life in Jesus. If you don't know anyone who knows Jesus Christ already, write to me via my website, RebeccaBauer.org, and we will make sure that you get some material to help you start your new life in Christ.

Interaction: The Grid and the Goal

"Type A"—that would probably describe me. Intense. Motivated. Focused. Persistent. Most important: *Gotta have a plan.*

All of you Type Bs: Before you decide that this won't apply to you because you aren't a Type A, I'm asking you to at least read this section. You may tweak it to suit your needs, or you may not use it at all. But I found that in grief, I forgot everything! I even wrote "brush your teeth" on my daily list because I was so scattered mentally and emotionally. The point being: Even if you aren't naturally a list-making, gotta-have-a-plan kind of person, these tactics may be helpful for you in this season of your journey.

So back to my plan: I approached grief in my usual Type-A way. Having been in ministry for a few decades, I knew that the average grief journey took around 24 months. So—me being me—I created a chart representing eight 3-month periods, and then I set goals for each quarter. For example, when Scott died, I was already slated for cataract surgery. While I delayed it, it still had to be done, so it went on the chart.

Another example: church. Because Scott and I were the senior pastors, the entire congregation was on this grief journey with me. I had lost my husband; they had lost their pastor. It was an extremely difficult season for all of us. Because I had thousands of people on my journey with me, however, I knew that I had to "ease" back into church attendance. So I gave myself a quarter to not be at every service—occasionally I listened online. Then I set a goal to be back at all of the services.

I had goals on the grid related to all of the major areas of my life: work, home, medical, financial, family, church. I predetermined when I thought I would be able to do everything.

A great idea. Or so I thought. I wound up not being able to keep up with my plan and had to slow things down. The upside of the grid, however, was that it *did* keep me aiming at a goal. (*That's important for a Type A!*) Probably for the first time in my life, though, I felt free to not be bound to the list. If I didn't meet a goal, I just moved it to a future timeframe. The grid guaranteed that I didn't forget important issues, and that I kept moving forward.

I also had a stated goal: to come out of this journey with the least amount of baggage possible.

The goal was kept short so I could easily remember it, but it did have a couple of additional thoughts attached to it. My loss was so sudden and far-reaching that I knew it could become the definition of my future if I wasn't careful. We so often define people by something bad that has happened to them! Just look at some of the people in the Bible: for instance, Mary Magdalene is always the one "out of whom [Jesus] cast seven demons" (Mark 16:9), even though she was delivered. There was also "Simon the leper," who I'm assuming had been healed if he was having a dinner at his house (see Matt. 26:6). A woman once asked me, "As a believer in Jesus Christ, when does the stigma of divorce finally ever leave you?" She had gotten divorced as an unbeliever and had been faithfully serving the Lord as a single woman for two decades. She felt that at some point, she should no longer be "the divorced woman." She was right.

Jesus doesn't define us by our pasts, and I didn't want to wind up defining myself—or letting other people define me—by something negative, either. On my journey, I didn't want to become "Rebecca the Widow."

I also discovered that there are fine lines between true grieving, grief avoidance and self-pity. I wanted to process the true baggage of the situation, completely and without the self-absorption that self-pity would bring, making the loss the center of my personal universe. My understanding of this part of the process was: *I wanted to cry every tear I was supposed to—not too many, which would give place to self-pity, and not too few, which would leave issues unresolved.*

While there were plusses and minuses to my "Grid and Goal" plan, I have to say that overall, it was positive and kept me forward focused. I would encourage you to take some time to begin to define where you want to head as you process your loss, whatever it may be. What do you want to come out of your journey with? (Or without?) What are a couple of things at which you're aiming for your new future? Are there things you would like to add, subtract or change about your life? Definition helps to get us on track toward the future as we process the past.

Note

1. My "Perfect Day" is not any big secret, nor would it work for everyone, because each of us would have a different perfect day. In essence, it is a day that runs smoothly, allows time for everything, and includes the little things (e.g., vitamins, etc.) that help me stay on top of everything.

WILL I STILL TRUST?

Choices: Will I Still Trust?

"Building where you believe" and "will I still trust?" can sound like related topics. Yet, for me, the issue of trust dealt with some different things:

- Was I going to be thankful?
- Was I going to give God the benefit of the doubt?
- Did I trust God with my life? Did I trust God with *Scott's* life?

Nehemiah 9:17 has been a significant Scripture in my life for a long time, but during my grief journey it became very important. One day as I was walking and thinking, I pondered the different responses people have to loss. Some people—many people—come out of the journey with a joy and appreciation for life that they never had before. That's what I wanted! Others, though, come out bitter and angry; they are resentful at anyone else's joy because something significant left their life. I had seen it happen to other people, but in the process of my journey, I didn't want to become a hard-hearted person (see p. 142). So I presented my dilemma to the Lord:

*How do I walk this awful road and not become
hard-hearted . . . or bitter . . . or angry?*

It was then that the Lord reminded me of Nehemiah 9. That chapter reiterates the journey of Israel in the wilderness, and lists all of the bad attitudes that they struggled with on their journey: Pride. Presumption. Anger. Murmuring. Disobedience. Rebellion. Every bad attitude is there! Verse 17 gives the root cause of their thanklessness:

They were not mindful of Your wonders.

I felt encouraged that if I looked for the kindnesses of God's hand in a stressful, frightening and sorrowful situation, it would help me to keep my heart soft. I began to look backward at the year before Scott's death—at all of the things that happened, the joys we had, things God said, trips we took . . . all of it. I realized that God—knowing that Scott's appointment was near—had given us the most wonderful year we had ever had together. Two of our children got married; we celebrated four graduations; there was a big family reunion for Scott's parents' fiftieth anniversary—we even rode jet skis . . . which was pretty brave for the girl who didn't swim!

I started a kindness list of things God had done for me, and I reviewed it regularly . . . because we forget. We don't mean to, but we do. The list got longer and longer. As I've walked the last decade, I've kept adding to it. The kindnesses of God are always around us. He is faithful and good. Circumstances change; life may not turn out the way we had hoped—but He remains the same. He is the only constant in life. And He is always kind. In fact, that's how Nehemiah 9:17 ends:

[He is] abundant in kindness, and did not forsake them.

All of this eventually brought me to the decision that I would give God the benefit of the doubt. This is actually a rule that Scott and I chose to live by in our marriage. Communication between people is not always perfect, so we decided early in our marriage that if we hurt each other's feelings, or if one of us didn't understand something the other person said, we would give each other the benefit of the doubt that it was unintentional.

Of course I don't believe that God miscommunicates; He is perfect. The only imperfect thing that happens in communication is on our side: *We* don't hear correctly. *We* don't understand what He's doing. *We* get our feelings hurt, so to speak. But I came to the conclusion, as I thought on His kindnesses, that even when I didn't understand, I would give Him the benefit of the doubt that His thoughts toward me were always good.

Your thoughts toward us . . . are more than can be numbered (Ps. 40:5).

[His thoughts are] thoughts of peace and not of evil (Jer. 29:11).

In the end, I had to decide:

> *Did I trust the Lord with my life?*
> *Did I trust Him with Scott's life?*

Believe me when I say, I have hashed this one out with the Lord! People were telling me that we "missed something." "We didn't pray hard enough." Some were even so bold as to suggest that Scott "must've had secret sin in his life." As I pondered this in front of the Lord, and looked at His kindnesses and lessons of the previous year, I knew it wasn't that we had missed something. This was simply Scott's appointment. The days that were written for him were completed.

It is appointed for men to die once (Heb. 9:27).

Your eyes saw my substance, being yet unformed.
And in Your book they all were written,
   the days fashioned for me,
When as yet there were none of them (Ps. 139:16).

This is sometimes difficult to accept for people of faith, who pray and believe God for change in the world around them. Healing of bodies. Restoration of families. Salvation of souls. Provision for those in need.

I believe we are called to pray for the world around us. But in this circumstance, I also discovered that, as people of faith, we tend to have a very poor theology of death. The Word says:

Precious in the sight of the LORD is the death of His saints (Ps. 116:15).

To be absent from the body [is] to be present with the Lord (2 Cor. 5:8).

To die is gain (Phil. 1:21).

I do Not view KAY's death AS Negative. I view it As her gain.

From our side of eternity, we view death only as a negative; and yet from God's side, He views it as:

Precious. Presence. Gain.

Why? Because His goal has always been to dwell with, in and among His people. Immanuel. God with us.

While we miss our loved ones—and it is certainly appropriate to love, honor and remember them—they have stepped into God's presence. Complete wholeness. Joy unending. Life everlasting. And . . . the next stage of the adventure of life in God. I don't know what God will have us doing when we get to heaven, but I don't think we're going to be sitting on clouds, strumming harps. God is a much better steward of His creation than that!

If I could trust the Lord with the issues of death, then I knew that I could also trust Him with the issues of life. He's a good steward of my life, too.

Do NOT QUESTION GOD—

Wrestling: Secret Things

I Never ASKED THESE QUESTIONS.

Somewhere along the way, almost everyone wrestles with the question "Why?" *Why did this happen to me? Why did Scott have to die? Why didn't God answer my prayer? Why wasn't Scott healed? Why—when he was accomplishing so much for the Lord—was he not given more time to do good work? Why?* And its variations: *Where is the "good" in this? Where do I see God at work? How is this "better"?*

In general, "Why?" was not a question I asked, because I knew that there was no answer to it that would satisfy me. Even if there was an answer I understood, it wasn't going to change the reality I was living with every day. Because I believe that

God sees a bigger picture than we do, my reaction tended to be more along the lines of: "I'd better see some purpose in this . . ." versus a plain old "Why?" Bottom line: They're probably the same question!

I came across a verse one day that helped me:

> The secret things belong to the LORD our God, but those things which are revealed belong to us and to our children forever, that we may do all the words of this law (Deut. 29:29).

In other words: There are things God knows that we will never know; but the things He's revealed to us? We're responsible for them.

Proverbs 25:2 says, "It is the glory of God to conceal a matter, but the glory of kings is to search out a matter." Therein we have the lifelong tension between wanting to figure it out right now, and God revealing things over time. He illuminates the words of Scripture, and suddenly we understand something we never understood before. It is the Spirit who reveals all truth (see John 16:13). God—like the good Father He is—reveals to us what we need. Not necessarily what we want.

When my children were young, they would occasionally ask me a question whose answer I knew they were too young to fully understand. So I came up with a response: "Are you sure you want to know that?" They quickly came to understand what I meant: "You are old enough to be trusted with an answer, but young enough that you should not have to wrestle with this information. *Do you really want to know?*" I believe that God relates to us in much the same way. He knows things that we do not, and He knows we aren't equipped to deal with even the knowledge of those things.

There are things I still don't understand about the "Why Scott?" "Why me?" and "Why now?" questions. Frankly, I will probably never understand some of those things. I've made peace with that—not in a resigned kind of way, but with the understanding that I'm not God, I'm not going to understand everything that happens, and if I fully understood everything, it would make me God's equal. He *is* bigger than we are.

Secret things.

you did —

In the aftermath of Scott's death, I also wrestled with: *Why didn't I get a miracle?* We were certainly praying hard enough! We had enough people praying. I believed—one thousand percent—that Scott would be healed. I did not see his death coming.

When I look back and wonder about the unmet expectation of the situation, I realize that I have too small a view of that, too. On the journey, I have found that my view of the miraculous has both expanded and contracted. The outflow of heart-healing in my life has increased my appreciation for the miraculous in everyday life. God's kindnesses are manifest in daily bread and new mercies. "Timing" or "coincidences" that could only have been orchestrated by His hand are evident. His sustaining power is seen in each day and each breath. Sunrise. Color. We typically don't view these as miracles, because they happen without our investment of faith or involvement through prayer. Yet neither the healing of heart nor the appreciation of life is a "lesser" miracle.

My view of the miraculous has also, in a sense, contracted. My belief in miracles has become different—not necessarily less expectant, but more accepting and trusting when God seemingly does not act. *Secret things*. I simply trust that He knows better, and I'm okay with the fact that I don't know. I don't have to have the answer to everything.

Miracles do not happen because you are "good." In fact, they sometimes happen for people who on my scale of things don't "deserve" them. It's the same quandary Jeremiah found himself in when he lamented before God, "Why does the way of the wicked prosper? Why are those happy who deal so treacherously?" (Jer. 12:1). There are things that do not make sense to us. Yet . . .

We don't see the big picture.

We don't see people's hearts.

We don't see what God is growing in people.

We don't see what God is orchestrating.

We don't see . . .

We want everything to make "logical sense" when some things only make "faith sense." We want formulas so that we know when God will work, how He will work, and that we can make Him work. But miracles do not happen because you have faith or know the right words to pray. God's workings—much less the God who performs them—cannot be formulized, or the hand of the God who performs them cannot be forced.

Does Jesus do miracles today? I believe He does. But of greater importance than the miracles is the fact that He is growing people of character. He is more concerned with us becoming like Him. While I believe that miracles are to be the expectation of every believer, and that God works in many miraculous ways in our lives, I have also come to the conclusion that continual, instantaneous miracles would remove our need for faith and growth. Though it has become a cliché, it is still a fact: Standing firm in adversity *does* make us stronger. If we defaulted to the miraculous in every situation, our growth in Him would ultimately suffer.

Scott's death—his passing into eternity to live in the presence of the Lord—has informed my view of how God works, but it has not weakened my belief *that* He works. My journey has forced me to look deeper at the Scriptures, to know Jesus better, to value life more, and to define what I believe. It has forced me to understand what is revealed in the Word so that I am responsible in how I apply it.

What I have come to believe is that the moment of Scott's death was not intended to be a miracle moment. We did not miss something; the devil did not steal something. That moment was intended to be a disciple's appointment of stepping into heaven. A miracle would have been the "happier ending." While I still pray for miracles, I am more patient with the secret things that I do not know.

Lesson: His Presence and His Voice

As a young girl, I was taught to live my life "in front of Jesus." It's a phrase my grandmother used, and it has impacted my entire life. It simply means choosing to do everything we do with the awareness that we are doing it with Him, with His eyes upon it, and accepting His input into it. It means living with an understanding that His presence is always with us and that He wants to make His desire and direction known to us—*in front of Jesus, so we can hear Him.*

Paul presents this same concept in this way: "Do you not know that your body is the temple of the Holy Spirit who is in you, whom you have from God?" (1 Cor. 6:19). We receive the Holy Spirit at salvation (see John 20:22), and in that moment we become God's "temple"—His dwelling place. His desire with all of His dwellings is to "meet and speak" with His people (see Exod. 25:22). Since *we* are now His dwelling place, then, He wants to "speak" with us, too. What does that look like?

The idea of "hearing God" is scary to some. They may have seen the concept used manipulatively, or they might think it means they will start hearing voices. Let me assure you that neither of those is what hearing God is about. God desires to encounter His sons and daughters because He longs to help us and equip us to live our lives in Him successfully. Let me offer a definition; when I talk about "hearing God," I mean one of the following:

- Suddenly knowing what to do in a situation.
- "Coincidences" that happen so often that they can no longer be coincidental.
- A phrase is impressed on my heart, and it helps to lead me along my path of serving God.
- A Bible verse comes to mind and perfectly applies to my situation.

In fact, I believe that the Bible is the only ground to base hearing God upon. It is *the* primary source, guideline and measure for anything that the Lord wants to say to us. That's why it is so important that we study God's Word and read it daily.

The challenge to living in His presence and hearing His voice is that in the middle of a grief journey, the emotions can be so overwhelming that trying to be in the Word can sometimes just add to the sense of overload. For months, I could barely read anything, not even my Bible. The words seemed to just bounce off of the front of my forehead. In that season, one of the primary ways that the Lord encountered me was through worship music—*a phrase impressed on my heart*. Morning after morning, as I stepped out of bed, it's as though a song greeted me—and those songs carried me through many days.

On Christ the solid rock I stand.
Blessed be the name of the Lord.
Grace alone which God provides . . .
You are my strength, my rock, my fortress, deliverer,
strong tower.

He met me. And He "spoke" through song.

There are other things I did to keep my heart strong and tuned to the Lord:

1. *Spend time in worship*. I've already mentioned worship, but let me add that I have found that it feeds my soul in a way that nothing else does. In the initial stage of my grief journey, I was usually too exhausted to sing along. Sometimes I was even too exhausted to listen. During that season, I could only play music very softly—but it still fed me. That over-exhausted stage didn't last forever, and though it still took a long time before I was able to sing like I used to, the simple act of inviting God to speak through worship—and the strength that it brought to my soul— was very real.

2. *Pray*. As with other areas of my life in the Lord, I was initially so engulfed in what had happened that my usual patterns of prayer and Bible reading were non-existent. But Romans 8:26 says that God

even accepts our groans as a prayer. How unbelievably kind God is! He knows we face difficulty in life, and at those points when words do not come, He accepts the heart-cries we direct toward Him. So don't stop praying just because you can't spend an hour on your knees right now. I grew to appreciate this Scripture verse because there were days when all I did *in front of Jesus* was weep. I believe He accepted those tears—those groans—as prayer.

3. _Listen to the Word_. When the words you try to read are bouncing off of your brain, listen. You can access the Word online, or you may have CDs of parts of the Bible. Ephesians 5:26 refers to "the washing of water by the word." I heard a speaker once say that wild animals, when they are injured, will get into a stream so that the water can cool and wash a wound. What a terrific analogy! In times of woundedness, get into the stream and allow the Lord to wash you with the water of His Word.

I found that the more I did everything in front of Jesus, the more I was strengthened to walk the road I was on—even when I was dealing with the life insurance people; even when I had to go pick up death certificates; even when there were people who were unkind (sad, but true); even when I had to pack up my husband's office.

I knew that if I was holding His hand and listening, I would make a successful journey through—*through!*—the Valley of the Shadow into Life.

Application: Finances

Dealing with the financial aspects of my life was a difficult issue for me, because it wasn't something I had ever done. This may not be a big issue for you; no two journeys look exactly the same. But perhaps you are liquidating a parent's assets, or dealing with some business issues that require more expertise than you have had in the past. While the specifics may be different, my hope is that the lessons I learned on my journey will help you to deal with the challenges you are facing. I give this example here to encourage you to look at the areas of your life that present a high learning curve.

Scott had always been the main wage earner; I had been a stay-at-home mom for (count 'em) 25 years! My husband highly valued the work I did, and I had a great "product" to show for all those years of investment . . . but it wasn't going to pay the bills. In the midst of processing the loss of my husband, I needed to get a job, and I was also suddenly responsible for paying the bills, dealing with the bank, filing the life insurance claim, and getting everything we owned transferred into my name. While not every family operates the way we did, almost everyone who suffers loss will need to learn new skills to function in their new life. This was mine.

Life Insurance

Being the economics major, Scott took all of our financial issues very seriously. One of the things he did every year was give me the "life insurance speech" when he renewed the policy. We were more keenly aware of this issue because Scott had a brother who died in a military accident, leaving a wife and two small children. As we watched our sister-in-law go through her process, we began to realize how involved it was. She told me once that for six months, she carried a briefcase of paperwork with her everywhere she went. I found that to be true as well; there is a lot of paperwork to process.

The life insurance speech always consisted of three parts:

- This money is not intended to be invested (though as it turned out, I was able to invest some of it); it is intended to be used.
- This money is intended to give you "a five-year bridge to a new life."
- This money is for: paying off a mortgage, getting the kids through college, and re-tooling so that you can earn a living.

The claim for the life insurance was, obviously, applied for very early; however, the actual transfer came after several months. That was my call, not theirs. The agent I was dealing with strongly encouraged me to get the money moved as quickly as possible, because it would earn more in an investment account than at the life insurance company. She told me that many widows delayed "moving the money." I understood why. Intellectually speaking, I knew the agent was correct. But emotionally speaking, the insurance money *felt* like it was still connected to Scott as long as I left it with the life insurance company. Once I moved it, it was just mine. Alone. And that felt terrible. When I finally wrote the check to move that money away from the life insurance company, it was so emotionally draining, I think that's all I did that day.

This particular action may not feel that "heavy" to you. But something else will. The point is to be aware of the things that feel that way on your journey, and be prepared emotionally to take those difficult steps forward.

The Process of Collecting the Information to Transfer Ownership

The very first financial thing that had to happen was simply beginning the process of notifying companies and accounts that there had been a death and that everything needed to be transferred to my name only. After I notified the companies, they sent back paperwork to be filled out and requests for any other information they needed. (Most of the documents had to be notarized before they were returned. See below.) Once all of this information had been returned, the changes were processed (see p. 167).

Transferring Names/Notary

About two months down the road, all of the new information had been collected, but the official transfer to my name had yet to be done. One thing I learned is that in the instance of a death, investment accounts can be moved without penalty. So this process allowed me to consolidate and streamline some of the financial aspects of my life. At the time of transferring ownership and meeting with a notary, all accounts were moved to one location.

Once all of the information had been collected, an appointment was made to meet with a notary and a financial advisor. In my memory, it feels like this meeting took about two hours. I don't know if it was shorter or not. But honestly, the emotion of processing all of the transfers made it a very heavy meeting for me. If you have to do this, be prepared emotionally, and consider taking a strong support friend with you. For a couple of hours, all I did was sign, notarize, and turn over a death certificate. Over and over again. It was an awfully hard meeting. But once it was done, my finances were streamlined in a very good way.

This is the main area of my life that made me feel like "a big girl" . . . probably because I had never done it before. If this is a part of your life that you need help with, line up the people who can help you. I had several friends who were involved in the finance or banking industries, and their help was invaluable. I will admit that, 10 years down this road, doing the finances still isn't my "warm fuzzy moment"—but I can do it!

Interaction: What's Meaningful for You?

The *way* each person grieves is as individual as each loss is. There comes a point when you have to decide what is meaningful for you—and then do that. For example, a friend of mine wears his father's lapel pin every year on Father's Day and on his dad's birthday. A niece used her dad's name as her son's middle name. A couple who were close to us would re-read Scott's memorial bulletin on the anniversary of his death. When my brother-in-law died, it was important to me that after his grave marker was set in place, I went to the cemetery and touched his name.

In regard to Scott, it has been important to me to take flowers to the cemetery each time we have a new grandchild born. Scott is buried near his brother, Tom, who was killed in a military accident in 1989. On two occasions, grandchildren were born to Scott and Tom on the same day, within minutes of each other! On those days I took flowers to both graves—to celebrate Joshua and Gabrielle in 2004, and Kai and Ava in 2012. A very sweet kindness of the Lord to two grandpas who I believe are celebrating together in heaven. (Are there thunder-sticks in heaven? If so . . . Scott and Tom have them!)

Maybe these aren't unique things, but they are specific to each of those people. Occasionally people would ask me questions about how often I visited the cemetery (not often anymore), or why none of my grandchildren were named after Scott (actually, three of them are), or if I had kept Scott's wedding ring (yes). They wanted my grief to look a certain way.

Be at peace. Your grief will have its own form of expression, and you need to do what's important to you. I have found that when emotions overwhelm, it helps to *do something to remember* rather than just *feel bad*. In those moments when you need to do something, here are a couple of ideas to consider:

- Are there things you shared with that person that were unique to the two of you? My brother-in-law and I both liked a certain kind of flower that no one else in the family liked. We kind of liked that about each other! So it was important to me to remember Tom by taking *that* kind of flower to his grave.
- I love the Jewish way of remembering those who have gone on ahead of us: lighting a candle on the anniversary of their death. Sometimes I do that on the anniversary of the person's birth, too.
- Writing a letter to the loved one can be very comforting. It provides an opportunity to express things that may have gone unsaid during their lifetime, or to acknowledge missing them when important events occur. While we cannot communicate with the dead (in fact, the Bible commands against trying [see Deut.

18:10-11]), writing down what we wish we could tell them gives us an outlet for our grief.

- While there are a lot of new things in my life, I am still surrounded by a lot of Scott's things, too. There is a balance between keeping and letting go. Maybe you've put away something that you need to get back out. I've done that with some of Scott's things. Something has been put away, and for a season I just need to get it back out. Back and forth. Ebb and flow. Grief is like that.

A Word About Cemeteries

I didn't know there was a "cemetery culture" until the first Christmas I went to Scott's grave. I bought a small poinsettia and took it out to the cemetery. When I arrived, however, the decorations on other graves were so far beyond my little plant, I was almost embarrassed! Entire Christmas trees—complete with decorations, garland and tinsel—were everywhere. I dropped off my poinsettia, then sat and looked around for a while. I watched a man down the slope from me setting up a tree. He got out boxes of ornaments and carefully placed them on the branches. When he was done putting the finishing touches on the decorations, he left. I wondered if this was a recent death in his family, so I walked down to look at the marker and check the dates. What I discovered surprised me. The death had taken place over 20 years before.

It was that moment that brought me to the realization that I wanted to remember and honor Scott with life . . . not by visiting "the burying ground." Again, this is all about balance. I do still go out there occasionally and make sure his marker is cleaned up and cared for. But the cemetery is not the place where Scott's memory is most marked. It is most marked in life. In children and grandchildren. In the "words of life" he taught each week at church. In the lives that were changed and grown in the Lord because of his teaching. For me, that is a better investment in his memory.

A Word About Writing a Grave Marker

I've read a lot of grave markers in the last few years! The grave marker next to Scott's says, "I'd rather be fishing!" I'm assuming that the writer of that marker hoped to communicate something *human* about their loved one—that they weren't just a name and a date. I can understand that. But when I had to write Scott's marker, I wanted to make it a testimony to a life well lived—and a testimony to what Scott had invested his life in: people. There was a word limit, so this was not a quick and easy task. But this is another way to honor the memory of a loved one. If this is a task you have to do, may I encourage you to consider: *a testimony to a life well lived.*

Part 3

THE HARD WORK OF GRIEF: WALKING THROUGH THE TUNNEL

5

WHAT WILL I SAY?

Choices: What Will I Say?

Everything had happened so quickly, I found I had a hard time making my mind accept the fact that he was gone. The week before Scott died, we had been in Europe, where he had been ministering at a conference and in several churches. To go from roaming the streets of Rotterdam with Scott to burying him just a week later was shocking.

My mind was having a hard time wrapping itself around how my life had changed.

I found myself, in the effort to comprehend this new reality, walking around my house, saying over and over, "My husband is dead; I am a widow."

This may sound crazy, but one of the additional phrases I said to myself was based on the widow-character in the musical *The Music Man*. In the story, everyone refers to her as "the Widow Paroo." So I would also say to myself, "I'm 'the Widow Bauer'."

As pathetic as all of this sounds, I think I truly was in shock. But one day, as I was saying this repeatedly to myself, the Lord stopped me. *"I want you to say only what's true."*

"What? Haven't You noticed, Lord? This *is* true! I *am* a widow! My husband *is* dead!"

"You're right," He responded to my heart. *"And I'm not telling you that you can't say that. But you also have to say the rest of the truth."* Then the Spirit began to remind me of some of the things that were also true:

- I will never leave you or forsake you (see Deut. 31:6; Heb. 13:5).
- You have a future and a hope (see Jer. 29:11).
- We don't sorrow without hope (see 1 Thess. 4:13, see also p. 41).
- There is joy in His presence (see Ps. 16:11; Jude 1:24).
- The Lord is always good . . . and always faithful (see Nah. 1:7; Deut. 7:9; 2 Thess. 3:3).
- He is my protector and safe place (see Pss. 33:20; 119:114).

Don't you just love the "alsos" of the Lord? He does not ask us to lie about our situation: "Oh, I'm just fine!" We are encouraged to be honest about it . . . but it has to be an honesty expressed in the light of His Word.

From that day on, my statements, as I grappled with my situation, became longer—and more complete:

- My husband is dead . . . but the Lord brings life out of impossible situations (see Jer. 32:17; Ezek. 37:1-14; Luke 1:37; 2 Tim. 1:10).
- I am a widow . . . but the Lord is faithful to widows (see Deut. 10:17-18; Ps. 146:9; Prov. 15:25).
- Life is changing . . . but God is my redeemer! (see Ps. 49:15, Isa. 48:17).

I had made another choice that would lead me forward: to speak the truth with hope, and in the light of the promises of God's Word. I was speaking life into my situation.

There were several other choices to make about "what I would say." One choice involved not using the things I said to garner pity for myself or try to get my way. I only did this on purpose one time . . . and was strongly reprimanded by the Lord. In conversation with someone, I blatantly played the widow card. I got what I wanted. But as I walked away from the encounter, the Lord spoke into my heart: *"You may never do that again."* Though I was speaking what was technically true, the spirit behind it was wrong and manipulative.

Another thing I tried not to do was to use all-inclusive words. They are rarely true, and they exaggerate the journey. Interestingly, the Greek word used for "truth" in the New Testament has to do with reality, accuracy and integrity. The use of that word calls us to accurately speak about the reality we are facing. All-inclusive words cannot do that. In the middle of loss, though, it's tempting to use them. The comment I found myself making was: "I've lost everything" (see p. 26). Other types of losses may draw out different all-inclusive comments that are not or should not be true: "Everyone is against me," "You can't trust anyone," or "I will never forgive that person."

There is only One who deserves our all-inclusive comments, because they are always true of Him; and that is the Lord. Consider these all-inclusive truths about God:

- He is always working on our behalf (see Ps. 121:4).
- He will always sustain us (see Ps. 55:22).
- He always leads us to triumph (see 2 Cor. 2:14).

- He is always sufficient for whatever we need (see 2 Cor. 9:8).
- He always lives to make intercession for us (see Heb. 7:25).

Choosing to speak truth is, at its root, choosing to do things God's way. In fact, the Hebrew word for "truth" (we looked at the Greek one above) literally means "firmness, faithfulness, reliability, stability, truth." A sure, firm, reliable and stable thing. If we're committed to building where we believe, truth becomes a very large component of what we're building and how we're building it.

Finally, the Bible offers a perspective on how we speak that should arrest our attention: It views the act of speaking as actually creative. In Jewish thought, once a word is spoken, it takes on a life and reality of its own. "Words" couldn't be "taken back." Look at what happened when Isaac blessed his sons (see Gen. 27:1-38). Although Jacob had taken the blessing by stealth, when Esau came in begging his father for a blessing of his own, Isaac said, "I have blessed him—and indeed he shall be blessed." "Your brother came with deceit and has taken away your blessing." And in response to Esau's question, "Have you not reserved a blessing for me?" Isaac responded, "Indeed I have made him your master, and all his brethren I have given to him as servants; with grain and wine I have sustained him" (vv. 33,35-37). In other words, the blessing Isaac had given to Jacob could not be taken back.

Viewing this account through our American, liberty-and-justice-for-all lens, we want to take this to trial, prove that Jacob acted deceitfully, and return the blessing to its rightful owner. But words don't work like that. They have the power to give or take life.

That makes a lot of difference as we walk toward the future. Consider what else the Bible has to say about our words:

A wholesome tongue is a tree of life (Prov. 15:4).

Death and life are in the power of the tongue (Prov. 18:21).

He who would love life and see good days, let him refrain his tongue from evil, and his lips from speaking deceit (1 Pet. 3:10).

[Jesus said,] "The words that I speak to you are spirit, and they are life" (John 6:63).

As you continue through the Valley of the Shadow, make the choice to speak life into your loss, and watch the redeeming hand of the Lord begin to work on your behalf.

Wrestling:
What Does Suffering Accomplish?

No one likes suffering. (Now, there's an understatement!) When my girlfriends and I were all having our babies, one of the expectant dads said to me, "Please pray that my wife has a fast labor; she just isn't into pain and discomfort."

I actually made no comment, but what I wanted to say was: "Right—because the rest of us really like it."

No one likes pain. No one likes discomfort. No one likes suffering.

But, as with labor, pain paves the road to bringing forth life. The bottom line is that adversity, suffering and pain ultimately produce:

Growth. Life. Fruitfulness.

We see this modeled in the life of Jesus, who endured incredible adversity, suffering and pain for us:

[God] made Him who had no sin to be sin for us (2 Cor. 5:21, *NIV*).

[He was] delivered . . . up for us all (Rom. 8:32).

Christ died for the ungodly (Rom. 5:6).

He . . . taste[d] death for everyone (Heb. 2:9).

But it all started with loss:

Let this mind be in you which was also in Christ Jesus, who, being in the form of God, did not consider it robbery to be equal with God, but made Himself of no reputation, taking the form of a bondservant, and coming in the likeness of men. And being found in appearance as a man, He humbled Himself and became obedient to the point of death, even the death of the cross (Phil. 2:5-8).

No reputation. Bondservant. Humbled.
Obedient. Death of the Cross.

He gave up everything He had.

We tend to have this mental picture that, yes, Jesus did become a man—but He was still "above" us, in the sense that He wasn't *really* quite human. *Right?* He probably floated a few inches above the ground. (He didn't *really* need to wash His feet.) He probably never sweated. (Have you ever experienced summer in the Middle East?) Or spilled any food. Or stubbed a toe. Did He ever accidentally step in donkey-doo?

Is that sacrilegious?

I don't think so.

If we really believe that we have a High Priest who can "sympathize with our weaknesses, [and who] was in all points tempted as we are, yet without sin" (Heb. 4:15), then we also have to believe that the things He experienced *as a human* extend beyond our mental preconceptions. His humanity extends to *everything* we experience as people. He came to show us how to live . . .

Every day. Here. On earth.

He knows what it's like to walk a lifetime of human existence; and it started with loss. But it didn't end there! Look at the conclusions of the passages we read above and we see what He gained:

We [could] become the righteousness of God in Him (2 Cor. 5:21).

He [could] freely give us all things (Rom. 8:32).

We [could] be saved from wrath through Him (Rom. 5:9).

For it was fitting for Him . . . in bringing many sons to glory, *to make the captain of their salvation perfect through sufferings* (Heb. 2:10, emphasis added).

For the joy that was set before Him [He] endured the cross
(Heb. 12:2).

Jesus thought that all the suffering He went through was
worth it, so that He could gain . . . *us*.

Does that give you hope for your journey?

It should.

Jesus has paved the way for us to successfully overcome loss,
and to see life come out of our pain. The author of Hebrews goes
on to say, "Consider Him who endured such hostility from sinners
against Himself, lest you become weary and discouraged in your
souls" (Heb. 12:3). And Jesus Himself told us, "In the world you
will have tribulation; but be of good cheer, *I have overcome the world*"
(John 16:33, emphasis added). He knows the road *through* suffering
because He walked it ahead of us. And because He overcame it, He is
there to walk with us on our journey so that we can overcome, too.

Look at how Paul addresses the issue of our suffering: "For I
consider that the sufferings of this present time are not worthy to
be compared with the glory which shall be revealed in us" (Rom.
8:18). The suffering we are living through now will pale in com-
parison to the outcome.

In another of his epistles, Paul says, "I also count all things
loss for the excellence of the knowledge of Christ Jesus my Lord . . .
that I may know Him and the power of His resurrection, and the
fellowship of His sufferings, being conformed to His death" (Phil.
3:8-10). As we walk through the "fellowship of His sufferings," we
come through it knowing Him better.

Peter writes, "May the God of all grace, who called us to His
eternal glory by Christ Jesus, after you have suffered a while, perfect, establish, strengthen, and settle you" (1 Pet. 5:10).

James adds, "My brethren, take the prophets, who spoke in the name of the Lord, as an example of suffering and patience. Indeed we count them blessed who endure" (Jas. 5:10-11). And look at who James's example is: "You have heard of the perseverance of Job and *seen the end intended by the Lord* . . ." (v. 11, emphasis added).

The outcome is worth the journey.

That I may know Him.

Perfect, establish, strengthen, settle.

The end intended by the Lord . . .

On this journey, I have wondered what it would be like if we always "got a miracle." What if we were granted the ability to get the answer *we* wanted—immediately and on our terms— every time? What if we knew some biblical abracadabra faith statement that would move God's hand *every* time? Sickness . . . gone. Provision . . . got it. Loss . . . turned around! We think that's what we want, but that type of answer would require no faith, no growth, no discipline, no commitment, no patience, no perseverance, and no need to hear God's voice.

As much as we may chafe under the heaviness of the journey, it requires us to lean into Him more than before, to learn more about Him, and to listen more closely for His voice. Suffering is a long and difficult road to walk. Jesus understands that.

But what comes out of that journey makes all the difference in our lives and our faith and our future.

Lesson: Grief Is My Job

During this season of my life, I viewed grief as my job. I've already said that I had a defined goal (see p. 30). Keeping our eyes on the place where we want to end up helps us to stay focused and moving forward. Still, there is the day-to-day reality of navigating through the process. There are some very practical lessons I learned that helped me to do both: to keep the goal in sight, but still deal appropriately with each day.

Fly into the Pain

I read once that you have to go backward in order to go forward.[1] When faced with loss, it can be tempting to simply leap toward the future and hope everything else will just "resolve." But the issue of loss needs to be faced head-on and dealt with if we are going to pursue the future in freedom.

The phrase I used for this process was "fly into the pain." That phrase came out of a conversation between Scott and his brother.

My brother-in-law flew helicopters for the Air Force. One day, in conversation, Scott asked him, "What do you do if you are attacked?"

Tom's answer was that missiles are usually set to go off at a specific distance, so when you find yourself under attack, you are supposed to turn your aircraft around and fly directly at the enemy. That way, you quickly narrow the distance, and the missiles fly past, exploding behind you.

Fly into the attack. Fly into the pain. That phrase came with the understanding that if I turned and faced the issue of grief, I wouldn't be caught in the middle of the explosion.

Brutal Honesty

Maybe on this journey we don't want to use the word "brutal"! "Intense" would also work. Bottom line: Be honest about what you're feeling. There are a lot of emotions flying around while you're in the Valley. *Grief. Fear. Doubt. Loss. Anger. Betrayal.*

As we've talked about before, the only safe place to deal with all of them is in front of the Lord. I thought I had done that . . . until I re-read my journal in preparation for writing this book. As I read, I couldn't help but notice how many times I wrote the words "I'm mad." Usually they were written in relation to things I now had to do because Scott used to handle them: the car, taking the garbage out, yard work, paying the bills, and so on.

I have to admit that there are moments when those things still make me mad! What I learned, though, is that God is not intimidated by our honesty. He would rather that we come right out and say what we think and feel, instead of hiding in the bushes like Adam and Eve did. He knows anyway. Our hiding does not keep anything from Him; it only encourages dishonesty in us.

The psalmists felt free to air all of their emotions in front of God:

- My life is spent with grief (Ps. 31:10).
- I groan because of the turmoil of my heart (Ps. 38:8).
- I am restless in my complaint (Ps. 55:2).
- I am weary with my crying; my throat is dry (Ps. 69:3).
- When I thought how to understand this, it was too painful for me (Ps. 73:16).

They even felt free to ask "why" and "how long" questions! (See Pss. 10:1; 42:9; 88:14; 13:1; 82:2.) And these were their worship songs![2]

Make Space to Grieve

In counseling people, I have sometimes suggested keeping an "emotion journal" in which they write in the presence of the Lord. This is not any different from what the psalmists were doing in pouring out their own emotions.

In a perfect world, every time grief overwhelmed us, we would be able to step aside, deal with it, and then move on. But in reality, that is not always possible. You may be at work. Or in the middle of dinner. Or teaching a Sunday School class. And suddenly—*there it is again*.

On my journey, whenever grief threatened to overwhelm me or tears were near the surface, I stopped right then (if possible) and dealt with it. I found that if I did that, I usually didn't completely fall apart and have an hours-long crying spell. In other words . . . the grief came out bit by bit, drop by drop, tear by tear, instead of in a tidal wave. Admittedly, we don't always have the luxury of stopping right then; but when I was able to do that, I found that the grief remained a little more manageable.

To compensate for those times when we can't "stop right then," I would recommend having a set time each day when you know that you will be able to be alone to journal, pray and pour your heart out before the Lord. Each time the next layer of emotion appears, it is helpful to know that you already have a plan in place to pour it out.

David writes, "Be angry, and do not sin" (Ps. 4:4). This implies to me that there are ways to process emotions that are and are not "sinful." Literally, the word used here for "sin" means to "miss the mark" or "miss the way." When we process our emotions with the Lord—in honesty, and making space for Him to be with us and search our hearts—we will not miss the way. We won't miss the way to wholeness. We won't miss the way to the future. We will not miss the way through the Valley.

Finally . . . Praise

Virtually every psalm that pours out emotion to the Lord ends with words of praise, hope, trust and faith. The psalmists processed what they felt, but they always came back to what they believed. They knew where to run . . . they knew to be honest . . . and they knew to return to praise. We referenced several psalms above that pour out emotion to the Lord; now let's look at what else the writers proclaim:

How great is Your goodness (Ps. 31:19).

In You, O LORD, I hope (Ps. 38:15).

Cast your burden on the LORD, and He shall sustain you (Ps. 55:22).

I will praise the name of God with a song (Ps. 69:30).

Whom have I in heaven but You?
And there is none upon earth that I desire besides You.
I have put my trust in the Lord GOD (Ps. 73:25,28).

When my husband collapsed at the end of a prayer meeting at our church, we were in the middle of singing a song based on Psalm 73:25. I began my journey with that verse, and I have completed my journey declaring the works of the Lord. No matter what we face . . . He is good, and He will sustain us as we process grief as our job.

Application: What's in Your Heart?

The Bible says, "Out of the abundance of the heart the mouth speaks" (Matt. 12:34). So I want to ask, "What's in your heart?" and "How is it impacting your journey?"

Several years ago, I was introduced to a book that explores the concept of survival in the wilderness.[3] Written about adventurers and explorers, primarily from the early to mid-1900s, this book shares stories of what these daring individuals did and how they survived when the unexpected happened—when a sudden storm hit while they were in the middle of Antarctica; when their ship was disabled on the open seas; when a member of their party was injured and they were unable to get back to civilization for help.

The book reviews the tragedies and triumphs of these amazing people. In the process, as the questions "Who lives?" "Who dies?" and "Why?" are asked, some unexpected life lessons are uncovered.

What the author learned is that the people who survived are the ones who didn't get distracted from the survival process. They stayed focused on what had to be done, they didn't second-guess past decisions, they were committed to bringing their companions through the crisis as well, and they were honest with the reality they faced.

Focus. Confidence. Selflessness. Honesty.

Ultimately, survival came down to "what was in the heart"— not simply the issues of provisions or skill or equipment, but the resolve and inner conviction that kept each person *forward focused*. It is no different for us. What is in our hearts will flow out and impact our journey through the Valley.

This concept should not surprise us, because we see it everywhere in life. We see it in how people face any kind of crisis. Studies have shown that people who face a medical challenge—cancer, surgery, long-term convalescence—are more likely to make a full recovery if the situation is faced with a positive attitude. Any time there is a natural disaster and we see people interviewed on the news, we can see it before our eyes: the difference between those who are already focused on recovery and the future and those with a hopeless, "all is lost" attitude.

This concept of "what's in the heart" is also significant when applied to a journey of loss, grief and recovery. We want to make it to the good future God has for us!

The Highway of Holiness

One of the things was were discovered to hinder survival was when people found themselves in a situation where the map they held in hand didn't seem to match the surroundings they were looking at. Rather than rely on what the map said, the temptation was to try to make the two "realities" coordinate. This is called "bending the map." Confusion and fear would set in as people tried again and again to make the two line up . . . until they found themselves hopelessly lost, and their survival was in question.

On a journey of loss, we face the same disorienting scenario. We have spent our lives seeking to live as "good Christians," and suddenly "how our lives are turning out" and "what we're promised in God's Word" don't appear to match.

Speaking the truth begins with looking honestly at the situation you are in. *Where are you today? Does it line up with the Bible? Are you continuing to "follow the map" and do what the Bible says?* As frightening as the journey may sometimes be, this is not the time to decide to do something contrary to what Scripture teaches us. The Word is our map. When we find ourselves in the middle of something that strikes fear into our hearts, our temptation is to rush in to fix it—by whatever means possible. Or we find ourselves seeking the false comfort of whatever makes us feel good at the moment.

Isaiah recognized this tendency in people when he wrote that there is a road "called the Highway of Holiness. . . . Whoever walks the road, although a fool, shall not go astray" (Isa. 35:8). *Don't be foolish and bend the map!* Isaiah goes on to describe what the end of the journey will be for those who stay on the road: "They shall obtain joy and gladness, and sorrow and sighing shall flee away" (v. 10). The only sure thing to do that will get us to survival is to stick with the map—God's Word—and do what it says.

Following the Leader

Over the years, I've heard many people speak what is "their truth"—what they perceive is happening around them. But God calls us to speak *His* truth into our circumstances. The disciples responded to a life-threatening situation by presuming that Jesus didn't care:

Teacher, do You not care that we are perishing? (Mark 4:38).

Like the disciples, we so often leap immediately to fear and blame: "Jesus, I'm suffering! I'm afraid! I'm about to die . . . *and You don't care!*"

Jesus walks into the storm and says, "Peace, be still!" (v. 39). Notice that He deals with the storm and with the disciples separately. So it is with us. He speaks to whatever our personal storm is, and then He speaks to us: Don't be afraid. Believe.

Throughout the Old Testament, we see the phrase "be of good courage"—the inverse of "don't be afraid." The Hebrew word for "good courage" means "to grow or become strong." This is a process. We often think that if we aren't strong today, we're just weak in general. But a lack of strength today does not mean we can't grow and be stronger tomorrow. The psalmist writes:

Be of good courage, and He shall strengthen your heart (Ps. 27:14).

What's in your heart? Be strong in the Lord. Stick with the "map" of Scripture. And believe the Lord to speak into the storm of your loss.

Interaction: The Challenge of Celebrations

One thing I remember hearing repeatedly is this: "Just get through the first year and then you'll be past all of the firsts." Well, this was only true with things that happened annually. As time went by, I discovered that there were many firsts that came after the first year: the birth of my first grandchild, graduations, conferences where I ran into people I had yet to see since Scott's death, my daughter's wedding. The list could go on and on. There will always be things that take place and make me think, *Scott was supposed to have been here for that.* The fact is, there will be "firsts" for the rest of my life.

Once I realized this, I could look ahead and prepare for the things I saw coming up. I could emotionally brace for them, and make plans regarding how I would handle certain aspects of different events. For example, my parents' fiftieth wedding anniversary took place about eight months after Scott died. The original plan was to have couples walk in together (my sister and her husband, my son and his wife, etc.), with an announcer introducing each couple. Well . . . the idea of my having to walk in by myself not only sounded bad to me but also would have been a difficult moment for many people present. This was supposed to be a celebration! Thinking ahead regarding events helped me look for potential places I might be vulnerable—and take steps to avoid unnecessary pain. When a "first" snuck up on me, it was harder.

The first year, of course, did have its own dynamic. We made sure we always had a plan for those special days that we knew would be especially difficult. For instance, the first Christmas was only two months after Scott's death. We decided we would start a new tradition, so we made reservations for Christmas dinner on board a ship at the Long Beach harbor. It sounded like a lot of fun, and there was nothing about it that would remind us of past Christmases. It would be something completely different.

Unfortunately for our plan, one of my sons had to have an emergency appendectomy shortly before Christmas, and then my other son and my daughter both got the flu. Clearly no one was interested in eating dinner onboard a ship! We cancelled our reservations and wound up barbecuing chicken in the rain. I suppose that wasn't like any other Christmas dinner we had had before either, but it certainly wasn't the one we had planned!

As you face the first year, look ahead to the holidays and significant family events that you know may be a challenge. Birthdays. Anniversaries. Valentine's Day. Come up with a plan so that you can be emotionally ready for those days.

As you move beyond the year of firsts, there are things to consider as you face those dates over and over. They will come up every year, and while it does get easier, there will be times when one of them suddenly hits you in the heart again. Sometimes those dates make sense and sometimes they do not. For example, the year my daughter had her first baby was a difficult year for her. She missed her dad. This made sense because she wished her father could be there to see her son. Then, there was one year when the anniversary of Scott's death was hard for all of us, though there was no logical reason that it should be.

Here are some questions to ask yourself as you look ahead and move toward the future:

- How should your loved one "be incorporated" and remembered for certain events?
- What anniversaries are going to be significant long-term?
- What upcoming events might bring up emotion?

How should your loved one "be incorporated" and remembered for certain events? Over time there have been several events that we felt needed to be handled in a way that included Scott, remembering that he is the "father" of our family. One of these was my daughter's wedding. She wanted a way to honor her dad, yet not make him the focus of the day. This was a sensitive situation, but my daughter came up with some very sweet ideas of how to do this. Of course, he was a part of her wedding video, but she also had a bouquet of flowers placed on the parents' row honoring Scott. My two sons walked the bouquet down the aisle and placed it at the same time that the parents were all seated.

I created my own personal tradition of taking flowers to the cemetery when each grandchild is born. Usually no one is with me, though several times I have had a grandkid with me when they are having a sibling being born. It's a very poignant juxtaposition of life and birth, remembrance and death, to be dropping off flowers at a grave while a child is running through the grass nearby. Decide what is significant to you, and remember your loved one with honor and love.

What anniversaries are going to be significant long-term? I don't know that Scott's birthday will ever go by without my remembering it. I'm so thankful that he was born, and that he was in my life! But when that day rolls around, some years are easier than others. You already know that I like to plan ahead! On Scott's birthday, there are several things I always do; they have become my own kind of tradition for that day. I call Scott's parents. I have something for dinner that Scott liked (German food!). I usually talk to all of my kids on that day.

What upcoming events might bring up emotion? There were a few things that brought up a lot of emotion for me. One of them was going to church every week. My husband was also my pastor, and every Sunday I could picture him up there preaching! Eventually (about five years after Scott's death), I did feel that it was time for me to attend elsewhere. I think it was healthy for me. And now, at my new church, my oldest son is one of my pastors!

Planning ahead, though it helps, doesn't eliminate every difficult moment. My sister-in-law told me that once, 16 years after her husband died, she was watching a Memorial Day parade, and everything hit her again. The losses we experience in life leave a mark on us that will impact us for the rest of our lives. Plan now to make those moments times of honoring and remembering, not just times of emotion.

Notes

1. Peter Scazzero, *Emotionally Healthy Spirituality* (Nashville, TN: Thomas Nelson, 2006), ch. 5.
2. See also Psalms 6:6; 31:13; 38:17; 44:24; 116:3 for more examples.
3. Thanks to Dr. Jonathon Huntzinger for his insights into these concepts, and for introducing me to the book *Deep Survival,* by Laurence Gonzales (New York: Norton & Company, 2005).

6

WHO AM I NOW?

Choices: Who Am I Now?

It was July 3, 2006, and, though we hadn't talked about what everyone would do for the Fourth of July holiday, I presumed (first mistake!) that all of my children would be coming to my house for the day. After all—*it's what we used to do.*

For the first several years following Scott's death, I didn't invite anyone over, because it was just all so sad. Emotionally, I couldn't do it. Now I was suddenly ready to have holidays at my house. The problem was that I hadn't told anyone that!

As I called each of my children, I discovered that they all had other plans for the day. As I hung up the phone after the last call, a wave of self-pity swept over me. I'm pushing fifty, and I sat there feeling old, discarded and sorry for myself.

Fine, I thought. *I'll just stay home and clean the attic.* (Yes, I did actually say those words!)

As I sat there, working up a pretty good pity-party for myself, it was suddenly as though I could see my future—going one of two ways, becoming one of two people.

In my mind's eye, I saw one woman who was old, gray and bent over, huddled in her home for all of the one-day holidays for decades to come. She puttered around her house, doing tasks that were nice to have completed, but weren't really necessary. Her life sure was neat and clean. Small and boring, but neat and clean! The mental picture reminded me of a story I had read years before, in which a woman, due to her disappointment and hurt, isolated herself from everyone and made her home on a tiny island. She was completely self-sufficient and never had to see anyone. She lived alone . . . and eventually died alone. The author writes, "'Twas a small place to make a whole world of."[1]

The other woman looked young (for her age!) and energetic. She was active and kept busy outside of her home. She was engaged with people, full of life, filled with joy, strong and adventurous. She was productive, and she made a difference in the world around her. She was creative and outgoing. She was *fun!*

It was as though the Lord stood those two women in front of me and asked, *"Which one do you want to be?"*

Well . . . that wasn't a hard choice to make! I said "Yes!" to becoming the second woman. I also decided that I was going to say "Yes!" to the next person who called and invited me to anything. Ten minutes later, a girlfriend called and invited me to a Fourth of July event—a parade out in a "cowboy town" in the California desert. I said yes. We had a great time. It was out of my comfort zone. I was intentionally choosing to become:

Engaged with people . . . Full of life . . . Filled with joy.

On the journey of loss, it is very easy to default to becoming the woman who was arthritic and gray. Many times that *is* how it feels. But remember . . . we're building in the world we believe,

You choose what you want to Be

not the world we feel (see p. 55). So that day I chose a different road. The experience reminded me of a verse I had read in the psalms, describing what God wants to do in people as they grow older:

> Those who are planted in the house of the LORD shall flourish in the courts of our God. They shall still bear fruit in old age; they shall be fresh and flourishing, to declare that the LORD is upright; He is my rock, and there is no unrighteousness in Him (Ps. 92:13-15).

I liked the idea of being "fresh and flourishing" . . . it sounded like that lady I had decided to become! I did have to chuckle to myself when my study Bible noted that "fresh" meant "full of sap." Humorous terminology aside, I knew I was making another choice for life. Besides, if "full of sap" described someone who was fruitful, productive, fresh, flourishing and lively . . . well, then "full of sap" was what I wanted to be!

Just like I had a choice between the two women I could become, the apostle Paul offers a similar choice to all of us. In Galatians 4, he talks about the two covenants of God, comparing them to the bondwoman (Hagar, or the earthly Jerusalem) and the freewoman (Sarah, or the heavenly Jerusalem).

Paul writes that "the Jerusalem above is free, which is the mother of us all. For it is written:

> 'Rejoice, O barren,
> You who do not bear!
> Break forth and shout,
> You who are not in labor!

For the desolate has many more children than she
who has a husband'"
(Gal. 4:26-27; see also Isa. 54:1).

On July 3, I had felt barren, unfruitful and desolate. The Greek word for "desolate" means "solitary, lonely, bereft." The Hebrew term, while it means the same thing, also carries the idea of being stunned by the desolation. By July 4, I was breaking forth in praise, waiting to see what the Lord would do next . . . how He would use my life in this new season.

It was part of my process of going from wife to widow to . . . Rebecca.

Around that same time, I had to fill out a form that asked my marital status. It's funny how responses to things change over time. At the beginning of my journey, I *wanted* to check "widowed." I was in such deep grief that I felt compelled to tell people that my husband had died. My loss felt overwhelming.

A few years later, I felt frustrated by the question. "Married" had just one box to check. You either were or you weren't. But if you "weren't married," you had to choose "single," "widowed" or "divorced." I found it strange that people wanted to know why I was not married.

On *this* day, I found myself staring at the boxes. Technically, yes, I was widowed. But in reality, I generally did not feel that deep grief anymore. Finally, I checked the "single" box, turned in my form, and left the office.

As I walked down the steps, I realized that I had just made another choice: I had chosen not to have my life defined by death anymore. I had been widowed; my husband had died.

This was a fact, not my identity. Yet again, I was making the choice for life. *Fresh and flourishing. Full of sap.*

Wrestling: Lazarus

While Scott was in the hospital (a total of about 40 hours), dozens and dozens of people wrote me notes or left phone messages telling me that the verse they felt the Lord impressing on their hearts was from the story of Lazarus's resurrection:

This sickness is not unto death . . . (John 11:4).

But Scott died.

In the days that followed, I felt perplexed about how things had turned out. I believed God's Word, and I knew the people who had quoted that verse to me. They weren't superficial people who thoughtlessly threw Scripture verses around.

One day I was thinking about the Lazarus story, and I remembered the first time I heard it—in Sunday School. I remembered the flannel-graph pictures my teacher used to present the story. There was a picture of Jesus and Martha, and there was a picture of a tomb with a mummy inside of it. (As a matter of fact, about a year later, one of my kids was getting ready to teach this same lesson in Sunday School and was cutting out the flannel-graph pictures . . . *and they were the same ones!* They're still around!)

As I continued thinking about these pictures, I began to imagine my story: It was as though I was standing there with Jesus, and Scott was in the tomb. In my bewilderment, I cried out to the Lord, "If You weren't going to resurrect him, why did you impress that verse on the hearts of all of those people?"

His answer came immediately to my heart: *"You have the people in the wrong places."* With those words, the picture in my mind changed to Scott being with Jesus, and me being in the tomb. The Lord continued, *"And now I'm telling you . . .* come forth!"

This moment was a turning point in how I viewed myself and my future. Feeling that the Lord was calling me to *come forth* caused me to realize that He still had a purpose and a mission for me. He had a call on my life and something for me to do. In our marriage, my husband and I had shared a purpose and mission together. When he was suddenly gone, I felt adrift in regard to my own life-purpose; but now I knew that:

> *God still had a plan for me.*

In the days and weeks that followed, I studied this passage of Scripture (John 11:1-44) in more depth. There were three phrases that stood out and helped to direct me toward new purpose in my life.

The first "phrase" is a word: "believe." The word is used six times in the text (see vv. 15, 25, 26, 27, 40 and 42)—five of those times, it is spoken by Jesus. I had already chosen to "build where I believe," but Jesus' repetition of this word called me again and again to *believe Him*. Not just to believe *in* Him unto salvation, but to believe that He was present in my situation; that He would impact my circumstance; and that no matter how "dead" things looked, He would bring life out of it.

Interestingly, one of Scott's sermons was on this passage. In that sermon, he challenged our congregation with these words:

> Could it be in the steps of our own disappointment that some of us become so philosophical—so "theologically

pure"—that we've lost the sense of anticipation that God wants to do something right here, right now? The fact is that wherever Jesus is, a miracle is in process. Either it's about to happen, or it is currently happening, or it just finished happening! Every time Jesus shows up on the scene, there's a miracle.[2]

And Jesus cries out, *"Come forth!"* And He calls us to:

Believe. Believe. Believe.

The second phrase that stood out to me were Jesus' poignant words as He made His way with Mary and Martha to Lazarus's tomb: "Where have you laid him?" (v. 34). *Where is the grave, Martha? Where have you buried your brother, Mary? Where have you laid your future to rest, Rebecca? Where have you put your dreams? Your hopes?*

Until I was challenged by that question, I had not realized how many things I had allowed to drop out of my life. *Curiosity. Adventure. Exploration.* I didn't realize how comfortable I had allowed myself to become. In my defense, let me say that when you're raising children, there is a season to stay home—to focus on "the nest." But now the Lord was reawakening things in me as He called me toward a future that had been redefined by events I never could have imagined. *Where have you laid your dreams, Rebecca? It's time for you to let Me bring them back to life.*

Finally the phrase "for the glory of God" (vv. 4 and 40) brought a definition of purpose for the future. Life really is all about Jesus, because He's the only One who can give it. Another of Scott's sermons came to mind, in which he said:

All we do, all we say, all for Jesus, all the time.[3]

The fact is that the verse that begins with "this sickness is not unto death" ends with "but for the glory of God" (v. 4). Everything is to be done for the glory of the Lord. In sickness and health. In life and death. Whether we're abased or abounding. In gain or loss. In silence or sound. Dealing with the past or facing the future (see Eccles. 3:1-8; Rom. 8:37-39; Phil. 4:12). Regardless of what we each face, the outcome is always to be for His glory.

Paul exhorts us, "Whatever you do, do all to the glory of God" (1 Cor. 10:31).

In the case of Lazarus, the "glory of God" was manifested in a physical resurrection. In my case, the "glory of God" was shown through a scared widow choosing to step into the future God was opening to her. Make no mistake: Lazarus was no less frightened and overwhelmed when he stepped out of the tomb—stinky, dressed in grave clothes, and surrounded by people weeping and wailing—than any of us are when we take the first tentative steps toward our future. What will the glory of God look like in each of our lives? We will never know until we answer His call to:

Come forth!

Lesson: I Am Complete in Him

Our culture lives with a lot of movie theology—beliefs that stem from the entertainment industry rather than from the Word of God. One of the things our culture has come to believe in is the concept of finding the one person who "completes you." It sounds so romantic . . . but it just isn't true.

The Bible says that God made people "good." In fact, when Adam was going to be "made one" with the woman God created for him, he had to become "incomplete" by donating a rib. Before that . . . he was complete. When God created people . . . He made them good. Complete. Perfect. The crown of creation. Of course, once sin entered the picture, we were broken like everything else in creation—and in our brokenness, we do need completion. Scripture makes it clear, however, that we "are complete in Him" (Col. 2:10).

In other words, people who are unmarried (or, in Facebook parlance, not "in a relationship") aren't "halves" running around trying to find their other half. It is God—and only God through Jesus Christ—who can complete us.

I've thought about this a lot, because Scripture also teaches that when we marry, we "become one" with our spouse (see, for example, Matt. 19:5). This is about more than just sex! Oneness of purpose and goals, joys and sorrows, commitment and values are all intended to be part of becoming one over a lifetime. In fact, Jesus said, "What God has joined together, let not man separate" (Matt. 19:6). The *King James Version* uses the more poetic phrase "put asunder." Either way, being joined together as one means not being separated—not just physically, but also emotionally, spiritually or intellectually. *We think the same. We believe the same. We're headed in the same direction.*

Like Adam, when we choose to become one with another person, we lay aside something of ourselves—and so does that other person. One and one don't equal one. To become one with another requires the willing sacrifice of our individual dreams, hopes and goals to embrace a newly defined set of shared dreams, hopes and goals. It's an exciting, wonderful choice to make.

But it costs something.

When Scott and I got married, I laid aside some things that perhaps I would have held on to had I never married. Scott did the same. Together we embraced and defined a whole new entity that was *us!* We were each complete before we married; as a married couple, we were a complete unit. It wasn't until Scott died that I ever felt *incomplete*.

All of this led me to ask the question: What happens when God "puts it asunder"?

If I believe that Scott's death was his appointment—that the days of his life were completed, and that his home-going was ordained by the Creator—then I also have to believe that God knew that the marriage would be "put asunder." My husband and I would be separated from each other. I realized that it was at that point that I felt like I became "a half." On this journey of loss and recovery, I discovered that I had a lot of things to wrestle through as I walked the road to becoming "complete in Him" once again.

First, I had to accept the current status of the marriage.

This was not an easy place to come to—being married to Scott had encompassed my entire adult life! Yet, Romans 7:2 makes it clear that while a woman's husband lives, she is "bound by law" to him; but once he dies, that tie is broken. Paul uses an interesting phrase: "she is released from the law of her husband."

As surely as "being one" means more than sex, being released from the law of my husband meant more than just the changing of my marital status. Suddenly, I was the one in charge of the home. I was the one making the decisions. I was the wage-earner. It was not just a matter of being "alone," but of learning to lead, too.

For his part, Scott now dwells where there "is neither marriage nor giving in marriage" (see Matt. 22:29-30). These verses brought me to the awareness that *marriage is confined to time*. Once we step into the realm of eternity, there are other relationships that become our priority. We now stand in the presence of the God of the universe, and He supersedes all other loves and loyalties. I love how *THE MESSAGE* version renders this same pair of verses:

> You don't know your Bibles, and you don't know how God works. At the resurrection we're beyond marriage. As with the angels, all our ecstasies and intimacies then will be with God.

This does not imply that we won't have fellowship with, or recognition of, one another in heaven. It's simply that the refining, perfecting and self-sacrificing process of marriage will be fulfilled another way.

The second question I wrestled with was:
If you are the remaining spouse, are you just a
"half" for the rest of your life?

Absolutely not! It may feel like that for a time, but our redeeming God is always committed to seeing wholeness brought to whatever brokenness happens in life. Whether the redemptive need is for salvation, or provision, or healing, or seeing heart-wholeness come after a loss—*God is committed to making us complete.*

[We are] confident of this very thing, that He who has begun a good work in you will complete it until the day of
Jesus Christ (Phil. 1:6).

May [you] stand perfect and complete in all the will of God
(Col. 4:12).

May [you] be perfect and complete, lacking nothing (Jas. 1:4).

What about your life-purpose? How has that changed?

My call to ministry happened when I was nine years old. I felt that
the Lord was calling me to be a pastor's wife. Since part of my call
and life-purpose was defined by being a wife, I have to admit that
there was a period of time during which I felt very aimless. What
was I supposed to do? As I moved forward in my journey, I learned
that the God who redeems is also perfectly capable of providing a
new mission statement for the next phase of life. Over time, He re-
directed me to a new life-purpose and passion that wasted nothing of my past—educationally or experientially—while embracing
a new future.

Paul writes to the Corinthians, "Become complete" (2 Cor.
13:11)! If you are following Jesus Christ, you are on the road of
"becoming," and on that road, He is fully committed to "complet-
ing." What He has begun, He will finish. "Loss" is not the end of
your story.

Application: Wedding Rings

It was 1990 and I was sitting next to my sister-in-law at the airport.
I was getting ready to head home after a visit. She was in her early

thirties and had two young daughters. Life had turned upside down for her the year before when her husband died. As we were waiting for the plane, she kept twisting her wedding rings, which she still wore. Finally she asked, "What do you do when you're ready to stop wearing your wedding rings?"

Who would have ever guessed that years later I would be asking the same question?

Along the way, I have discovered that what a widow does with her wedding rings is highly personal and highly significant. My sister-in-law eventually decided to have the diamonds from her rings put into a necklace, so though she stopped wearing her rings, she still had a significant memento. When I stopped wearing my rings, I put them into the safe, but took the diamond Scott had given me for our twenty-fifth anniversary and put it into a different ring that I wear occasionally. A friend had her and her husband's rings soldered together and threw them into the sea.

For each of us, the decision about what to do with our rings represents a corner turned in our journeys and in how we now view ourselves. It is not an easy decision to make, because those rings carry so much meaning.

I remember the day Scott and I went engagement ring shopping. He couldn't believe I fell in love with the very first one! I never got tired of it. I never lost it. I never wanted a new one. I loved my wedding rings.

No . . . coming to the decision to no longer wear them was not easy . . . and, like everything else, it was a process.

When Scott died, I put his ring on along with mine. I had left Scott's ring on his finger until all of the machines had been turned off and his heart had beat its last heartbeat. The doctor's prognosis the day before had been very, very grim. But I was determined to leave that ring on his finger. It was my faith statement that I was believing for healing. I was taught, by my parents and by my husband, to believe for healing until there is no life remaining. I did that.

And then I left the hospital wearing his ring.

Until that day, the only time I ever wore Scott's ring was at the beach. We had a friend who had lost his wedding ring *four times,* usually at the beach. So I insisted on wearing Scott's ring at the beach. I wasn't taking any chances with losing it!

The day I left that hospital, wearing Scott's ring seemed like the right thing to do. Maybe it was sorrow. Maybe it was desperation. Lots of emotions were swirling around inside of me. But when I thought about it, those emotions didn't seem to fit the choice I had made. Finally I realized that for me wearing Scott's ring represented covenant, commitment, vows before God. Promises made for a lifetime . . . and now kept and completed.

It represented everything we had built and believed in, because our covenant wasn't only with each other, but also with Jesus. He was our foundation. He was our source. He was what we built upon. In committing to each other, we had fully invited Him into our lives and into our marriage. We had committed to Him. He was everything! The rings represented the foundation of our marriage. We knew that emotions come and go, beauty and youth come and go, and difficulties in life come and go. To weather those changes, we would have to be built on something bigger. We would have to be built on Jesus!

Of course, the ring also represented faithfulness and trust. For me, Scott was a true picture of Jesus' love for the Church, and because of that model of faithfulness, I knew how to relate to Jesus as my Bridegroom. What Paul wrote in Ephesians 5 about how husbands are to love their wives like Jesus loves all of us, to cherish and nurture them, and to present them beautiful and pure to the Father—well, Scott did all of that for me.

When I put his ring on my finger that day, all of this was wrapped up in that action.

But the ring story didn't end there. In fact, my rings became a symbol of walking my entire journey. There came a day when I "knew" I was no longer to wear his ring, then a day when I moved my ring to my right hand, and finally a day when I had my diamond reset and did not wear my wedding rings again.

Another process. Letting go. Forward focused.

I was putting a period on Scott's and my story.

That's why the ring decision is so difficult. It is the acknowledgment that something has come to an end. As much as Scott and what I learned from him still influence my life every day, as much as I see Scott in his children . . . and grand-children—and as much as I celebrate his life—the marriage has come to a conclusion.

I already mentioned that the diamond I still wear from time to time is the one Scott gave me for our twenty-fifth wedding anniversary. As we were coming to that celebration, he asked me if I would like a bigger diamond. I said no. I loved my rings the way they were, and they were filled with sentimental value.

He bought it anyway, because, he said, "Our future is bigger than our past."

This is why I wear that diamond. If I am building where I believe, then my future is always bigger than my past . . . no matter what has happened in the past.

If being widowed is the journey you're walking, there will come a day when you will need to decide what you will do with your rings. Until then, enjoy them and all that they have represented in your life. When the time is right, you will know what to do . . . and that will be another step into your future.

Interaction: Redefinition

Life had changed so dramatically that as I began to rebuild my life, I also had to take time to discover who I was now. I will admit up front that some of this felt a little bit like being a teenager again! There were days when I experienced the same kind of angst about myself that I had felt back then. Who was I now? Who was I becoming? Who was I "without Mom and Dad"? (That's the teenage question, of course! But the same concept applied now.) There were days that felt confusing because so much change was happening in my life. I was unsure where I was going to aim for a future career. I had always been defined by the people and tasks in my life . . . in the best possible way. Now, suddenly, *everything* that defined me was changing at the same time!

- At work—I was no longer "the boss's wife"; I was one of the staff members.
- At church—I was no longer "the pastor's wife"; I was one of the congregants.
- As a mom—all of my kids were getting married and leaving home.
- As a wife—I was now a widow.

It was *all* different!

In fact, part of my process of being "redefined" involved dropping all of the definition that had been part of my life before. As I said, I had been defined by the people in my life. Not by requirement, but by relationship. I was Jack and Anna's daughter, then I was Scott's wife, and then—shock of all shocks—I was walking away from a Sunday School class and hearing someone say, "That's Brian, Kyle and Lindsey's mom."

While I was proud of all of those relationships and all of those people, my life no longer involved any of them on a daily basis. I was no longer the kid living with her parents, the wife living with her husband, or the mom living with her children. I lived alone. I went to a job every day. I went to school.

The Lord challenged me in this season to learn to be content with "just being His daughter."

Beyond all other relationships . . . this was the one that mattered the most. The challenge came to a head one day when I was supposed to be co-presenting at a conference. As my co-presenter and I were walking to the podium, the person introducing us gave the oddest introduction. I don't know if he forgot that there were two presenters or what, but he introduced my co-presenter and then said, "Oh . . . and she's bringing someone with her." I guess I was "someone."

As I walked up to the podium thinking that this was the absolute worst introduction I had ever received, I also thought, "It's okay if I'm just introduced as 'someone,' because I'm also God's daughter. And that's enough."

Another strange redefining moment was when I decided to start going places by myself. One of my first forays was to

Disneyland. *I know. I know.* Total southern California stereo-type! But I have always loved Disneyland, and I didn't want to "lose" it. So I bought an annual pass and decided that for a year, I would go once a month *by myself.*

The first time I went, I decided to go on my absolute fa-vorite ride first—It's a Small World! As I was standing in line, waiting for my boat, the Disneyland "cast member" said, *over the loud speaker,* "Ma'am, are you with the people behind you? Or are you by yourself?"

So much for trying to be inconspicuously alone!

I survived "the happiest place on earth," and went back sev-eral times. Part of "redefinition," for me, meant that I needed to learn to be comfortable by myself, and to learn who I was by myself.

Finally, redefining meant that I needed to get out of my comfort zone. One of the ways I did that was shopping. Yes . . . shopping. (Not necessarily buying!) Instead of just trying on what I was used to, I would choose outfits that were outside of my comfort zone to see what I might feel comfortable in for this next season of life. I'll admit right now that some of the ensembles were downright laughable! Some just felt like cos-tumes. But I found that the simple act of trying on clothes that pushed me out of my box (and incorporating a few unexpected items into my wardrobe) helped me to be open to new things in a very practical way.

Trying new things extended to other areas outside of my comfort zone—different tastes (I had always been a wimp about trying new food!), and colors that I had never worn or decorat-ed with. I took some classes to stretch my thinking. All of this contributed to my redefinition process.

There was another thing that I tried on, so to speak. I "tried on" various careers by doing a little Web searching, looking at school possibilities, and reading some books. Of course, I prayed about this, too. But as each idea was researched, and then discarded, it helped refine and define what I wanted to do with my life.

Being God's daughter. Being comfortable by myself. Getting out of my box.

All of these things helped me to walk toward who I was becoming in a new season of life. While the process did have some angst attached to it, in the end it was a lot of fun to see how God was bringing together the pieces of my past and the pieces of my future into a whole new life.

Notes
1. Willa Cather, story title unknown.
2. Quotation from a sermon at The Church On The Way, Van Nuys, CA, on April 9, 2000.
3. Quotation from a sermon at The Church On The Way, Van Nuys, CA, on October 5, 1997.

7

WHO ARE MY FRIENDS?

Choices: Who Are My Friends?

"People" are a part of my journey that I don't think I did particularly well. Maybe no one does. I realized partway through the process that I had some decisions to make in regard to people, but the muddle of the immediate circumstance created some muddle with people, too. In retrospect, if there is any one thing I would say about this aspect of the process, it would be: *Give people the benefit of the doubt.*

The fact is, as you walk through the Valley, people will come and go in your life. You are changing. Your life is changing. Your dreams and goals are changing. While some people will embrace your new life with you, others will not be able to.

Many of the people in my life were encouraging as I took steps forward—from the smallest steps to the biggest ones. They even offered moral support for steps that seem silly now but felt *huge* at the time! My daughter sat with me while I made my first online purchase. (It was for her wedding gown, after all!)

But there were other people who flatly told me that I needed to stay the same; they wanted my life not to change. That just was not possible. "Life had changed, but without my permission."[1] Unfortunately, over time, these people faded out of my day-to-day life. This wasn't because of animosity on anyone's part; it was simply that they were unable to imagine a different future for me.

What was harder for me were the people who suddenly disappeared from my life. At first, I was offended. I had already lost so much. Was I going to lose friends, too? I finally came to realize that this "sifting" was a natural part of the process. It was not possible to go into a new life with the same group of people. This happens at many milestones of life: going away to school, getting married, or moving to a new town. Life changes; people change. This was one of the choices I discovered I had to make. Was I going to take the natural sifting process personally and hold grudges? Or was I going to hold people with open hands, and love and embrace them whenever our paths *did* cross?

Another thing that was difficult and that I initially found strange was that slowly my group of friends became primarily single people, where before I had spent most of my social time with married people. For a while, I was also offended by this. Was it because my marital status had changed? Like it or not, intended or not, I felt shunned. Again, over time, I came to realize that the issue was something much more easily explainable, and that it was never intended by anyone to be hurtful. It was simply schedule based. I was now working during the daytime hours when I used to get together with my friends. In the evenings, they were, of course, at home with their husbands and children—a demand no longer present in my life. If I wanted to have dinner with friends after work, I needed to find people who were available in the evenings. That happened to be primarily other single, female heads of households—like I was now. What I had originally taken offense at was simply part of accepting the realities of my new life. No one was intentionally rejecting me.

To my chagrin, I also discovered later that there were people who, shortly after my journey of loss began, had their own begin. One friend was in a terrible accident, involving months of healing and physical therapy. Another lost a parent shortly after Scott died. They were processing their own journeys now. Years down the road, when we all began to compare notes, I was shocked to discover some things that I had not even heard about when they happened. I was so focused on my own journey that their losses didn't even cross my radar.

I needed to give people the benefit of the doubt. For the most part, everyone was just processing the best they knew how. I learned lot, though.

Primarily, I learned *how easy* it is to make things about . . . me, and how easy it is to let offense creep into my heart. While loss and grief must be walked through, they can also become incredibly all-consuming. We begin to look at everything through the lens of our own loss. But we need to make space for others who are just trying to process their own journeys. There are things that will happen that feel like they were intentionally done to us, but in reality they were not. This is another place of choosing to build where we believe—giving people the benefit of the doubt—rather than building where we feel.

I discovered that there were people I had hurt along the way, as well. There were people who wanted to help, people who wanted to be close, people who wanted to offer comfort. While I was busy being all-consumed with my journey, I had not noticed, and had therefore not accepted what was offered to me. *While I was busy being offended by some people, I had offended others!* I never intended to hurt anyone, but there were people I had cut off by my words or actions, and I had some relationship mending to do. Over time, those relationships have re-entered my life, been healed, and found solid footings for the future. But it took time. And, like with any apology, I've found that the best way to approach relationship mending is with humility and genuine love for the individual.

Wrestling: Job's Friends

If your journey has been anything like mine was, you've had a few of "Job's comforters" come calling on you. Some people come to comfort, and it truly is refreshing. But when you read through the book of Job and see some of the things his comforters said to him, it's not hard to recognize some of the things that are being said to you.

They were said to me, too.

This kind of "comfort" is hard. It isn't comforting. It seems more accusing. On page 37 we talked about two-ways theology. This is clearly what Job's friends believed! (See Job 4:7; 8:20; 36:6.) Rather than sympathize with Job, they told him everything they perceived he had done wrong. They were trying to answer the question "Why?"

Job was in a terrible situation:

- He had suffered financial collapse. (Think: the stock market crash of 1929.)
- Then he got word that all of his adult children—*all of them*—had perished in a disaster. (Think: the sinking of the Titanic.)
- *Then* he suffered a painful and debilitating disease. (Think: stage 4 cancer.)

Any one of these situations would be incredibly painful, and Job was dealing with all of them at the same time. I have a lot of compassion for Job. Who knows but that his disease was a stress response to everything else that was going on? The last straw, so to speak, was the words his wife said: "Why don't you just curse God and die!" (see Job 2:9). Job *did* challenge her on that statement, but I have also thought she has been unduly criticized for her words. I've heard her used as an example of an unsupportive wife, or someone who didn't have much faith, or who was just an angry, bitter woman.

In actuality, she was probably a woman in deep grief. Her children had all just died. While Job was dealing with his own grief, she was dealing with hers. And the husband who had been her strength and support through the years, suddenly wasn't. He was sick! She didn't know what to do. If you listen hard, you can hear the wail of anguish: "*Job! We've lost everything! We've lost everybody! All that's left for us is death! Why don't we just throw in the last towel we're holding on to and give up?*" She was a woman in despondency.

Grief can do that to you.

Then the friends show up. I would like to think that they would have been more compassionate than they appear to be. The fact is, however, that until you've walked the road of loss, you don't understand it. You think you do. I thought I did, when as a pastor's wife I would seek to comfort people. Now I look back and wonder how effective that ministry actually was. I hope they at least felt the love of my heart toward them. But I have to admit to myself, there are probably some who were glad when I walked away.

Because I didn't understand.

Job's friends didn't understand either.

Maybe the same is true of some of your friends. But they're doing the best they can—just like you are. Let me share two things I learned along the way that helped me in those moments when people said the wrong thing:

1. First, people really believe they are helping. Despite some of the decidedly unhelpful words spoken, and even though I was relieved when some conversations were over, people truly believed that they were offering something that would help me. I needed to choose to give them the benefit of the doubt.

2. What is offered to anyone on a journey of grief and loss is no different from what was offered to Job. Human beings are no different now than they were then, and we all default to the same responses to loss:

   • "Here's why this happened . . ." (See Job 8:3-6. In this case, Bildad was telling Job why his children had died.)

   • "Here's what you need to do now . . ." (See Job 22:21-26. I don't know about you, but I often felt that people treated me like I had lost my mind, not just my husband. And often they would want to talk about things that weren't any of their business. *How were my finances? What was I doing with Scott's personal belongings?* Questions that should never have been asked.)

   • "You're stubborn and God is chastening you." (See Job 15:25-26; 22:4. When in doubt, blame the bereaved. Or at least that's what it felt like . . .)

- "There's sin in your life ... you need to repent." (See Job 4:7-8; 8:18; 22:5. Always helpful.)
- "God did this." (See Job 4:5,9; 20:29.)
- From the bemoaning pessimists: "Life is just hard . . . then you die." (See Job 15.)
- "Forget your misery." (See Job 11:16.)
- My favorite: "If you were righteous, God would work for you." (See Job 8:6. As if God would ignore someone because they sinned. I seem to remember reading some-where that "while we were yet sinners, Christ died for us" (Rom. 5:8). God doesn't ignore us; He comes to redeem.)

I'm not saying all of this to mock people, but to point out that people feel a desperate need to figure out why the loss happened. They want to understand the reason for it. They're wrestling with what they believe, while you're wrestling, too. I have had all of the things above said to me, and in virtually every case, my friends believed they were offering something that would truly help me. I chose to accept what they said based on their heart-attitude rather than their words.

The words can hurt; I won't pretend any differently. But I want to encourage you to accept people's involvement based on their intention. As human beings, we often do so poorly when we intend so much goodness! I'm no different. Even after having walked this journey myself . . . I know I have said the wrong thing to people who were grieving. The difference now is that I have learned to say less, and to recognize the pain in their eyes more quickly.

Lesson: A Soft Heart in a Hard World

When you are walking through the Valley of the Shadow, you're walking through a very hard world . . . and a very hard season of life.

Our culture talks a lot about the "hardness" of life. We attend the "school of hard knocks," live "between a rock and hard place," and discover that there are no "hard and fast rules." We meet people who are as "hard as nails," drive a "hard bargain," and are a "hard act to follow." We encounter circumstances that are "hard to swallow," and we know people who have fallen on "hard times." We're "hard pressed," "hard up," play "hard to get," and need "hard cash." Along the way, we run into hard voices, faces, attitudes . . . and hearts. Out of sheer self-protection, our tendency is to become hard ourselves: We take a "hard line," develop hard feelings, and in the process become hard-hearted. Of course, we know without being told that this is not what the Lord wants for us. But on the trip through the Valley, and in having to deal with people who are well-meaning but not always helpful, it's easy to begin building walls of self-protection. Before we know it, we've developed a hard heart.

On my journey, I described the people I protected myself against as people who were "emotionally unsafe." I'm sure you understand that description. These were the people who poked and prodded at my heart, or who wanted me to "stay the same" and therefore hindered me from moving forward, or who simply said things that hurt.

One day, the Lord challenged me, pointing out that my list of emotionally unsafe people was getting pretty long. In other words, I was distancing myself from more and more people—and the long-term impact of that in my life, I realized, was unforgiveness. I knew I had to do something about that. I repented before the Lord for those attitudes, and I began to intentionally seek out some of those people to renew relationship. *They* didn't know they had been on my emotionally unsafe list; but I do know that they felt my distance. As I began to renew those relationships, I found that the majority of the people were now "safe." I took that to mean that the issue was actually probably mine from the start, but I was in such a fragile place that I needed the distance at the time.

What I learned was that while I may have initially needed tight parameters around people while I healed, left untended it turned into a heart issue in my own life that I needed to deal with. It was time to expand the parameters of my life. Bottom line: No matter what any of us go through, we never have the luxury of allowing hard-heartedness and unforgiveness into our lives.

Scripture says a lot about hard-heartedness; probably the best-known hard-hearted person in the Bible is the pharaoh of the Exodus. I've often heard people say things like: "I don't understand why God hardened Pharaoh's heart. Did God only love the Israelites? That doesn't sound like the God I know." But if you read the whole account (Exod. 4:21–14:8), you'll find that the entire process began with Pharaoh hardening his own heart time and time again. This teaches us a very sobering lesson: We can harden our hearts so often and to such an extent that the Lord simply gives us over to our own choices.

Matthew 19:8 tells us that hard-heartedness is the spirit behind divorce ... or any separation of relationship for that matter: separation in marriage; separation between ethnicities; separation between friends; separation between nations. But Jesus came to break down the wall of separation and "[make] both one" (Eph. 2:14). While we divide ourselves from others through hard-heartedness, God's desire is to unite people, and to bring healing to every relationship.

As you walk through your journey, are there people with whom you need to renew relationship?

Hard-heartedness is also the spirit and attitude behind lack of belief (see Mark 16:14), lack of understanding (see Mark 6:52), rebellion (see Heb. 3:8), deceitfulness (see Heb. 3:13), and unwillingness to give (see Deut. 15:7). All of these attitudes can hold us back from stepping into our futures. No wonder the Lord calls us to a more responsive way of life! But how can we foster that openness? How can we have a soft heart in a hard world?

First, break up fallow ground (see Hos. 10:12). Sometimes we just need to be honest about the hardness of heart that we have allowed, and then intentionally begin to break up those places and deal with them. Have we fostered unforgiveness toward anyone? Or anger? Where have we offended someone else? The first step to keeping our hearts soft is digging up hardness.

Digging things up isn't enough by itself . . . the Lord also calls us to repentance. Romans 2:4-5 tells us that "the goodness of God leads [us] to repentance," but when we have a hard and unrepentant heart, we treasure up judgment for ourselves. God doesn't just lead us to repentance that leads to salvation . . . He wants to lead us to repentance every day. So as you dig in your heart, and the Lord brings things to light, make sure that you not only restore relationship, but also repent before the Lord. After all, all sin, no matter who else is involved, is ultimately against God (see Ps. 51:4).

Second, be with the Body. Hebrews 3:13 tells us to "exhort one another daily . . . lest any of you be hardened." We hear the voice of the Lord through one another. Are you meeting with the congregation? Are there believers in your life to whom you are accountable? Are you accepting the exhortation of others . . . or are you trying to justify and explain away your own behavior? We are given to one another as safeguards.

Finally, begin to give. Deuteronomy 15:7 cautions us against hardening our hearts to the need of those around us. Where do you see need? Do you volunteer in your church or community? Do you give in tithes and offerings? Giving will always keep us softened in compassion, as it opens our hearts to the world around us. All of life is a balance. There are times, as we've discussed, when it's important to pull in the boundaries, living in "emotional intensive care." But the boundaries cannot stay that small forever. Are you at a stage in your journey where it is time to look at a little expansion? A little reengagement?

On part of my journey, the Lord told me to "remember My kindnesses" (see p. 74) to keep my heart soft. It was a simple reminder that even in the school of hard knocks, even between a rock and a hard place, if I keep my focus on *the* Rock who supports me, my heart will stay soft . . . even in a hard world.

Yours will, too.

Application: Setting Parameters

Early in my journey, I noticed an interesting phenomenon: People would purposely avoid talking about Scott, and if I brought him up, they would change the subject. I think they were trying to avoid a topic they assumed was painful for me. In actuality, however, remembering Scott was never painful for me. (The fact that he was gone was, of course, a whole other issue.)

This is one of the things that I spoke with a counselor about. I didn't know what to do when the people around me were clearly uncomfortable with my new situation in life. The counselor told me that I was going to have to be the one who set the parameters for what was okay to talk about. I needed to help people be comfortable with me, let them know what my current interests were, and tell them what the Lord was doing in my life. They knew how to relate to me the way my life was before, but they were unsure now.

To be honest . . . I was unsure, too! I was trying to figure out what my new life was going to look like. I still felt a little fragile. I was also a bit in disbelief that I had to be the one to do this! After all, I was the one whose life had just turned upside down. Now I had to do this, too? The answer to that is: "Yes . . . because you're the only one who knows what you can handle." Sometimes setting the parameters required that I cancel something. There were times I would commit to something, but when it arrived, I just knew I didn't have the fortitude to do it. So, I did cancel a few appointments. Until you are out of emotional intensive care, this is the way it will have to be. As you get healed and strong, this will no longer be an issue for you.

As I evaluated the situations I was running into, I developed ways to deal with each one. I would plan things to talk about with a certain individual or in a certain situation. If a situation that was uncomfortable for me happened more than once, I would pre-think a plan for "the next time."

The people closest to me, I could simply tell, "This is okay; this is not okay." Because they were familiar with my everyday life and the things I was facing right then, they were able to hear and respond to specifics.

Some people would only talk to me about indirect issues of my life. By that I mean that they would not ask me how I was, but rather how my children were. They would ask when one of my kids was graduating, but would not ask me about my job. They would ask about grandchildren, but not about anything regarding my future. In other words, they were comfortable asking about things that would be of interest to me, but they were not comfortable asking about my personal life. With people who reacted this way, again, I pre-planned. If I knew they would ask me about my grandkids, I would also be ready with a piece of personal information. I was trying to help define for them what was and was not okay to talk about. While some people asked questions that may have been too personal, others avoided making conversation.

Other people needed reassurance that I still cared about them and wanted them in my life. I didn't just love them because I had been the pastor's wife and it was "part of the job." I loved them for them. So, sometimes I would just walk around the sanctuary before or after a service and hug people. We were all on this journey together, and I wanted them to know how much I appreciated and needed their presence. Initially, though, I needed to keep these encounters brief. I set that parameter because I was the only one who could define how much time I was ready to spend interacting with people.

If I had to go to an event by myself, I would have a mental list of things to talk about with people. If these were people I rarely saw, I wanted to give them the most positive answer to how God was walking me through my circumstance.

There were also some parameters I had to set with regard to what I would not allow in my life. At one point, several single men in the congregation started hanging around after services "to talk." I was not comfortable with this, so I asked several friends to be aware and help me get to my car after services. (The desire for companionship will be talked about in chapter 8.)

There were also occasionally people I had to limit my time with because they wanted to dwell on the negative aspects of this journey in a way that slowed my progress rather than enhanced it. There were even some people who tried to make me cry! (As if weeping were the verification of either my grief or my love for Scott.)

If this went on, I would not commit to a lunch or other extended visit. Rather I would communicate via email, or schedule something that would have a specific end time because of another appointment. I was not being unkind; I was simply recognizing that I was in emotional intensive care. It wasn't forever. As my life became more defined and I became emotionally stronger, I didn't have the need to do this.

Very rarely, I got blunt and just asked someone to stop something. For example, one time a woman got very aggressive with me over the fact that she thought I should be dating. I actually did not disagree with her, but neither was this something I could just make happen. God opens that door in His own time. She wasn't happy with that answer, however, and she kept pushing on the topic. I finally told her that I needed her to stop. I said, "I'm going to ask you to stop now. I don't disagree with you, but there is nothing to be done here except pray. I would appreciate your prayers about this, but I need to not talk about it anymore."

It is hard to set parameters around your life; it is hard to be this bold with people. I recently spoke with a woman who had had major surgery. The people surrounding her were so desirous of helping her that they were actually wearing her out! At her current stage, she still needed more time to sleep and rest. I encouraged her with the same words the counselor had shared with me: You have to be the one to set the parameters, because you are the only one who knows what you need and what you can handle.

Interaction: Building a Support System

The Broadway hit song "People," from the musical *Funny Girl*, says, "People who need people are the luckiest people in the world." We've looked at some of the difficult aspects of dealing with people on the journey, but the fact is, we wouldn't be able to make it through the Valley without a lot of people walking along with us.

Forming Your Team

We need people on the journey with us. My experience was that several people immediately emerged as people who were emotionally safe, trustworthy, and ready to take the time necessary to be with me for the whole journey. In "track and field" lingo, these people will be your anchors.

There will be others who are like a relay team. They may be there for one lap, but not necessarily the whole race. That's okay. It's a fallacy to think that if people are not available for the whole journey, they aren't sincere. The relay team helps to bring fresh energy to the journey, provide insights for that season, and give the "anchor people" a break. This is certainly not unworthy, and we need to accept the fact that not everyone who walks the journey with us is there for the whole thing. It's okay. They are doing the job the Lord sent them for. All of my kids ran track in high school, and they taught me that both the anchors and the relay runners are needed for a successful team.

My sister immediately emerged as my main anchor person. Though she had three young children at home, she made time for whatever I needed. In those first months, she went with me to the market, held my hand in church, and intercepted people she knew I was not ready to deal with. I don't know how she did it! The Lord gave her great insight and wisdom to walk my journey with me. She made sure I was not alone. Her family invited me on outings and brought cake for my birthday. After the kids were in bed, she occasionally just stopped by to chat, with the understanding that evenings were long and lonely.

She did this for months, and I am forever thankful.

Many others ran laps with me. Some even ran multiple laps, weaving in and out of my life for this years-long journey. To all of them I am grateful . . . because I could never have walked this journey without them.

Committees

I formed what I called "committees" to advise me on areas of life where I either needed help or needed to learn. Some of the committees were short-term. For example, I needed to move. We had been living in a parsonage that our church owned and provided for the use of the pastor. Obviously, I knew I would not be staying there. The Church Council graciously gave me up to a year to move, but I knew I needed to get into my own "nest" as soon as possible, so that I could hunker down and heal. So I formed a House-Purchasing Committee. I could look at a house and decide if I thought it was pretty, or if the layout seemed good, or if it had the right amount of space. But I didn't know what to look for as far as structure, potential hazards, and even neighborhoods. (My brother-in-law looked at street lighting, number of yard entries, and so on. I would know to look for those things now, but I didn't then.)

My daughter and I would go look at houses, and when there was one that I thought had "let's make an offer" potential, I would have the whole committee come take a look. They gave me the yes or no on location and structure. At one house, they discovered a crack going up the entire back of the house (most likely from our most recent earthquake), which I had not noticed. The day I found my new home, my dad (who was on my House-Purchasing Committee) walked in and started to weep—the peace in that home was palpable. Location and space were perfect. *This was it!*

Other committees were longer term. One of those was my Finance Committee. I needed them for quite a while. If the loss you are facing is death, there will be financial things to deal with. There are, of course, other losses that also involve financial decisions. If yours does, I would strongly encourage you to find people in your life who can advise you in this area. If the person-of-expertise is of the opposite gender, I would also strongly encourage you not to meet with him or her alone. You are in a state of emotional upheaval, and the other individual is your friend. This puts both of you in a potentially vulnerable situation. Head off how the enemy might try to add insult to injury by not even making that opportunity available.

Further down the line, I formed a Relationship Committee, made up of trustworthy women in our congregation who helped guide me into the scary world of dating. These sisters knew about every non-family-member male friendship in my life—whether I thought the relationship had romantic potential or not. I had not dated since I was 18 years old and got engaged! I needed help and guidance. (More on relationships on p. 164.)

Once you have your committee members in place, be accountable to them. You have brought them together to inform and advise you, but it may be tempting to talk yourself out of their advice if you don't happen to like it. You have brought them onto a committee because you trust them, so heed their advice.

When the Cold Winds Blow . . .

Technically, I did not work for the church my husband pastored. I was the pastor's wife, and I did a lot of work at the church as a volunteer; in fact, I was the Women's Ministries director . . . but as a volunteer. (Some people think that is not fair; however, what I liked about the arrangement was that it provided me the luxuries of not having to keep office hours, of being able to work from home, and of going to all of my children's activities regardless of what time of day they occurred.)

All that is to say that when Scott died, I didn't have a job.

Several weeks later, our Church Council offered me a position on the church staff. Because I was still spending most of my time at home, several of them stopped by to make the official job offer. One of the couples had gotten me an afghan, and they brought it with them. It seemed like an odd gift at the moment, but after we had talked about the business reason for their visit, they asked how I was. We talked about that for a few minutes, and then they brought out the afghan and wrapped it around me. They said that this was something they felt they were supposed to do. As they wrapped me up, they added, "This afghan is intended to be a reminder for you, that when the cold winds blow—*and they will*—there are people here who love you and are prepared to wrap you up and keep you warm."

Well, the cold winds *did* blow . . . and the people *were* there.

In the days that followed, I would need the presence of all of those wonderful, thoughtful, loving people in my life. I could never have made the journey without them. While there are times when we need to insulate ourselves, there are also times to step out—no matter how vulnerable or defenseless we may feel—and take hold of the hands of the Body of Christ.

I beg to differ with the song. We aren't "lucky" to need others . . . we are blessed, blessed, blessed to have them with us on our journey!

Note

1. Unknown.

Part 4

BUILDING A NEW LIFE:
STEPPING INTO THE LIGHT

8

WHAT WILL I KEEP?

Choices: What Will I Keep?

Charles Swindoll describes the choice of simplicity as one of the main disciplines of learning "intimacy with the Almighty." But, he cautions, "It is neither easy nor automatic."[1] It requires a choice.

In the Valley of the Shadow, some of the "simplicity" feels like it is forced upon you, because—well—you're in loss. In my loss, I literally had to downsize by half. A lot of things had to go to make my new life work.

This wasn't an easy choice, because when you are dealing with a death, "things" are what you have left. One evening, I was watching a movie with my daughter. One of the characters said, "Whatever can be lost . . . see that it's lost."[2] I immediately knew that I had to follow this same advice. In the movie, the characters were "lightening the ship, so that they could go faster." That's what my new life was going to require of me! I was going to be sailing toward new lands! That sounded exciting, but the first step toward dreams and adventure was to lighten my load (see p. 170). Lightening the load involves getting rid of things, and it also requires a new way of thinking, because choosing simplicity will "reorder your private life."[3]

Life in our culture is complicated and filled with stuff. We live in a consumer-oriented, materialistic society. Dissatisfaction with what we have is normative. Don't think peer pressure is only for children; adults succumb just as easily, wanting to make sure that they have all of the accoutrements that make life comfortable and display success. "What you have" is the measure of "who you are." You discover how much that attitude is prevalent in our society when you find yourself in loss. When you're in loss, the fact that you have less—that you have lost a person, a position, or some of the things you had before—redefines you in the eyes of others. The culture demands it.

The Lord never intended for people to live this way. The way of the Lord is simplicity. This part of my journey unearthed attitudes in me that I never knew were there. Most noticeable to me was the fact that I found myself wanting to hoard all of my things. *After all . . . this is what I have now. This is what Scott gave me. If I don't keep this, I won't ever have any more.* Well, of course, technically, I was right: I wouldn't be receiving any more Christmas presents or anything like that from Scott. However, the attitude of "hoarding because I will never have any more" is a dangerous one for believers in Jesus Christ, because it will always lead us down the road of self-sufficiency. The Bible tells us that no matter what we think of ourselves and our ability to provide for ourselves, it will never be enough. "Not that we are sufficient of ourselves . . . but our sufficiency is from God" (2 Cor. 3:5).

One of my greatest lessons of simplicity was that if my "plate seemed too full," I had probably put something on it that wasn't supposed to be there. Not only does our culture gather things, but it also gathers tasks. We rush around doing, when the Lord calls us to "be." I first heard Peter Scazzero use this phrase at a pastors' gathering: "The Lord calls us to 'be,' not to 'do.' That's why He calls us human beings and not human doings."[4] We not only let our possessions define our success, but we often also let our duties define our significance. All of these attitudes surfaced in me as I walked through the Valley of loss . . . and I discovered that God wasn't impressed. Not with my possessions, nor with my duties.

Paul writes about "the simplicity that is in Christ" (2 Cor. 11:3). The same word is translated elsewhere as "singleness of heart" and carries the idea of simplicity helping us to focus on what is truly important in our lives. That is *always* Jesus. When we multiply our things and our tasks, we can lose focus on Him, and put the focus on the trappings of our lives. We never set out to do that, but it can creep in anyway. Until many of my things and tasks were stripped away, I did not realize how much I had defined myself by those things.

In certain respects, letting things and tasks go is like fasting. Fasting from food reminds us of our physical frailty and our need to rely on God as our provider. Fasting from tasks reminds us that our strength is not in ourselves. Author Mark Buchanan points out, "We've not been still long enough, often enough, to know ourselves, our friends, our family. Our God. Indeed, the worst hallucination busyness conjures is the conviction that *I am God. All depends on me. How will the right things happen at the right time if I'm not pushing and pulling and watching and worrying?*"[5]

In Deuteronomy, the Lord actually warns Israel of their vulnerability—*our vulnerability*—to forget Him in the face of material success. "Beware . . . lest—when you have eaten and are full, and have built beautiful houses and dwell in them; and when . . . your silver and your gold are multiplied . . . and you forget the LORD your God . . . —then you say in your heart, 'My power and the might of my hand have gained me this wealth'" (Deut. 8:11-17).

There is no amount of life insurance or possessions or buildings that will ever make you feel so secure that you will feel that you can face the future comfortably during the journey through the Valley. There is no amount of *things* that will secure my love for or memories of my husband. It's because the "issues of life"—love, remembering, trust, contentment, simplicity—are the things that flow from the heart (Prov. 4:23).

When we simplify, we are actually investing in the "true riches" that Jesus talked about.[6] Our priorities change as we refocus on the things of the Spirit. Paring down forces a reliance on the Lord that we would not know any other way. Letting go of material things also helps us to let go of emotional baggage. There is an appropriate remembering of the past, but when the past is all we see displayed around us, it leaves no space for the future.

I began my journey with the stated goal of wanting to come through the Valley with as little baggage as possible (see p. 71). When I set that goal, I was only thinking of emotional baggage. I didn't realize how much physical baggage there would be, too. There was something about this part of the process that required a kind of surrender of *all* things to Jesus that I had never experienced.

Choosing simplicity helped me to do that.

Wrestling: Reaching Forward

Paul instructs us to "[forget] those things which are behind and [reach] forward to those things which are ahead" (Phil. 3:13). Isaiah writes, "Behold, the former things have come to pass, and new things I declare; before they spring forth I tell you of them" (Isa. 42:9). When we talk about embracing the future, it seems that there are equal parts of "letting go" and "reaching forward." We have to let go of the past so that we can embrace the future.

In the Old Testament, we see a picture of this as Israel crossed the Jordan into the Promised Land. They had completed 40 years in the wilderness (sounds much like a journey of loss), and were preparing to possess their future. They had also just suffered the death of a beloved leader, Moses. In the wake of this loss, they were about to move into the future they had been promised. As we read through Joshua 4–5, however, we learn about some significant events that took place to mark the change in their status. They were no longer going to be a group of nomads wandering in the desert. The Lord was taking them into a land of promise that would provide permanence in their dwelling situation, cohesiveness as a nation, solidarity in warfare, and unity in worship.

As the Israelites crossed the Jordan River, Joshua instructed twelve men to take stones to set up an altar. "Let this be a sign," he said (see Josh. 4:6). It was a sign of God's miraculous workings to get them to this day, but it also marked the break between what they had been in the past and what God was doing in their future. At this season on my journey, I felt directed to be baptized in water again. I do not recommend this to everyone, nor did I do it casually. I knew in my heart that this was to mark a moment of decision for me: that I was willing to let God work in my life in a way that would make me into a new person with a new life. As surely as baptism carries that meaning in a salvation sense (see Rom. 6:4), for me that day it also had ramifications for my grief journey. This may not be how you choose to mark this season of your life, but I would encourage you to do something that is of significance for you.

As soon as they were across the Jordan, Joshua instructed all of the men to be circumcised (see Josh. 5:1-8). Throughout Scripture, circumcision is a mark of accepting covenant with the Lord. Paul made this application in a New Testament sense (see Rom. 2:29) by saying that we are to circumcise our hearts. It is this heart-commitment to a renewal of covenant that is significant here. For Israel, in Joshua 5, there was a physical application. For the church in Romans, there was a spiritual application. As I continued my journey through the Valley, my covenant-renewal had to do with standing before the Lord in His authority as a single woman. I will freely admit . . . being single was scary to me, and I didn't feel qualified to lead a home or a family *alone*. There is a passage in Numbers 30:1-9 that talks about how Israel was to relate to a daughter in the house of her father, a wife in the house of her husband, and a woman who was widowed or divorced. According to this passage, the single, female head of household was accountable before the Lord for herself. Accepting that place was a moment of covenant-renewal for me with the Lord. Again—I do not want to impose my process on anyone else; I am merely giving examples of how I did things in my own life. May I encourage you, as before, to do what is significant between you and Jesus.

A third thing happened upon Israel's entry into the land: The manna stopped. Joshua 5:12 says that "the manna ceased on the day after they had eaten the produce of the land." God was now providing for them in another way. The Lord gives a grace for the journey of loss that is different from "grace for daily life." The psalmist writes, "The LORD is near to those who have a broken heart" (Ps. 34:18). This doesn't mean that His grace is any less present later, but it is different. His daily bread, fresh oil and tender mercies are daily blessings that all of us receive. But in a new season, something new is required of us—sowing and reaping, preparing and cooking, laying the table and presenting a meal. Our daily bread is not just lying on the ground outside of our tent anymore; we now bear a new level of responsibility. Once we step into the future, we are called to press into, accept and extend new boundaries as surely as Israel did when they entered the Promised Land. They pressed back the enemy and pressed into the new land—the new life—that God was giving them. In *King James* wording, Paul says that we "press toward the mark" (Phil. 3:14).

Interestingly, once Israel began to take possession of the land, there is a word that is used to describe the "reach" of the God-intended boundary for each tribe. The word *pagah* is used to describe *how far* the boundary was to go—how far their inheritance reached. It essentially describes the *bigness* of the destiny God had for them. That is true for us, too. God has a big life ahead for every single one of us . . . but we have to "let go" and "reach forward" to it.

In Isaiah 53:12, that great messianic prophecy, this same word describes the Messiah as an *intercessor*. He stood in the gap and interceded for us when we were unable to do it for ourselves. The writer of Hebrews affirms this messianic activity by pointing out that our Messiah, Jesus, "always lives to make intercession for [us]" (Heb. 7:25; see also Rom. 8:34). And He wants us to partner with Him. We can never do the kind of intercession that Jesus does, but we are called to "pray without ceasing" (1 Thess. 5:17).

> At His side, we step into a new season
>   Partnering with Him
>   Praying without ceasing
>   Eating the produce of the land
>   *Pressing forward into our destiny.*

Lesson: Letting Go—
How Do You Become "Not Married"?

If your journey involves the loss of "being married"—either through death or divorce—the desire for a future relationship is normal. God created us for companionship; the first relationship He set in place was marriage. But what I have found is that we need to learn to be "not married," before we can step into another relationship.

People tend to want to hurry this along, but give yourself time. I read once that it takes about a year for every five years you were married to fully heal from the loss of a marriage. On my journey, I found this to be an accurate timeframe. You may be healing from different issues depending on whether you lost your marriage as a result of death or divorce, but either way, give yourself time to fully process your healing.

Suddenly being single didn't make me feel single on the inside. I got married at such a young age that I didn't know how to be not married. This became a very large part of my journey, because—clearly—my husband was gone . . . I was no longer married. But my responses to people and situations were all still "married" responses.

How do you stop being married? *Feeling* married?

One example that struck me as particularly funny happened several years down the road. A guy actually made a pass at me

(Wow! *That* hadn't happened in a long time!), and I didn't even notice it! Or respond to it!

I'm sure he was devastated! (That's a joke!)

But my point is, it was a married person response. There were other things, too. No one knew how devastating it was to suddenly have no one who held me. Or held my hand. No one to partner with. No one to give to. I found that one of the things I missed most was simply buying a man's shirt. (Buying one for one of my sons just wasn't the same.) It took me a couple of years to stop using "we" language: "We're going to do this." "We're going to go on vacation." It was such a habit that I repeatedly said "we" when only talking about myself. I had to make a point to correct myself . . . but how do you break a 30-year habit? As with everything else . . . with intention. With decision. With choice.

I remember that there came a morning, though, when as I woke up and was slowing waking to my day, it suddenly hit me: *I don't feel like a wife anymore*. Then more importantly: *I don't feel like a widow anymore, either*. The enormous losses were being assimilated into my new life. More steps toward joy. No longer consumed with grief, I began to just feel like . . . me!

It was at that point that I began to seriously consider the possibility of getting married again. Did I even want that? Not everyone does; if you are one of those who does not want to be married again, that's okay. This is not a question with a right or wrong answer.

If you would like to pursue the possibility of being married again, however, I would strongly suggest the following:

First and foremost, I absolutely urge you to create a relationship committee (see p. 151). We all need people who are watching out for us, and who are not involved in the emotional aspects of a relationship. Bring trusted friends into the process with you. Dating again is not like dating before. A long hiatus from dating can impair judgment. We get lonely and date anyone. Or we get excited about going out with someone and put up with anything. I'm not even talking about abuse here. (If that happens, run and don't ever go back. That is always inappropriate in any relationship.) Rather, I'm talking about someone who does not treat you with respect or who does not value you.

Walk God's way sexually. That's probably enough said! But let me add that it is difficult to turn this part of your life off. Still, there are many who have walked this road purely. You can do it, too. The gift of preserving yourself in obedience to the Lord—whether you remarry in the future or not—is worth more than leaving pieces of your heart strewn around for the world's version of love or comfort. That doesn't last; God's way does.

Timing is everything, and the timing is God's. People often want to speed the timing up: sometimes us, sometimes others. Before I was ready to even consider the thought of remarriage, a lady at church announced to me that "God wanted to give me a new husband." Well—okay. But I wasn't even ready for the thought, let alone the reality. The disturbing thing was that when I verbally backed away from that topic, the woman just kept pushing. I told my sister later that I wasn't sure what the woman wanted me to do: take applications? This isn't something you can make happen. God either does it or He doesn't. The timing is His.

I once heard a saying that I loved: "Dance with Jesus, and when the right man comes along, He will let him cut in." It makes the point. We can make something happen if we try hard enough. We could even take applications! But, as Scott and

I used to tell our children when they hit dating age, "You don't need to date around. You just need God to send the one."

Application: Dealing with the Stuff, Part 1

Every loss involves some kind of paper processing. While I cannot talk about every loss, I can talk about the loss of death and what that involved.

The Paper Process

Death Certificates
I remember feeling that the life of my husband had been reduced to paper—letters, photographs, files, sermons, books . . . and death certificates. Everyone wanted one. And the process was so incongruous. Because our bank accounts were all joint, I could go into the bank and withdraw every penny without anyone questioning anything. But the big-box grocery store wanted a death certificate to remove Scott's name from our account. One of the gas stations wanted a death certificate. It was frustrating because there was no standard process.

Though there was no standard process regarding the death certificates, transferring everything into my name did basically involve the following steps:

1. Writing an initial letter informing the company of Scott's death.
2. Waiting to receive a return letter from each company telling me what their process was. Typically they would send paperwork they wanted filled out.

The key variables to look for were: (a) if they wanted the document notarized, and (b) if they wanted a death certificate. If they wanted a death certificate, they would indicate whether a copy or an original was required.

3. Then, of course, sending back all of the paperwork. The people who advised me recommended collecting all of the return letters from the companies and then going to a notary with all of them at the same time. This saved time and money.

The day I went to pick up the death certificates was its own kind of loss. There were things the death certificate "told me" that had bypassed my radar in the immediacy of everything that was happening when Scott was in the hospital. The death certificate, of course, indicated the cause of death. Though I *knew* what that was, seeing it there in black and white felt like I was reliving it all over again. In movies, at moments like this, vision goes black, or sound becomes distant. I always thought that was just for effect.

It isn't.

It actually happened to me as I sat in my car in the post office parking lot, reading Scott's death certificate. A very surreal experience.

Books and Files

Another large part of my paper process was cleaning out Scott's office at the church. His assistant, of course, had gone through things and taken out everything that would belong in general church files. It literally took weeks to go through every file. Every email. Every drawer. Every book. It was all gone through and processed. An interesting side issue that developed from the files was the realization that I was now the owner of someone else's intellectual property. Scott had several books in process, loads of sermon notes, and teaching notebooks for entire seminary classes. I have used many of these things for my own research, and I hope someday to publish some of his works.

Scott also had quite the theological library. Another big job. When I moved, there were 40 packing boxes full of books. Before I moved anything, however, I wanted all of Scott's books to be embossed. He had a very cool embosser for his books; he just never used it! So I got it out and embossed everything. Many of the books went to my children, while others came home with me. While I've added supplemental volumes to the sets, they will always know which ones were their dad's, and which ones were added later.

Sympathy Cards and Letters

And the cards! Admittedly, we had a large congregation, but it took almost a year for me to read and respond to all the cards and letters that people sent. Emotionally, I could only read so many at a time; one day, I sat down to read, burst into tears at the first card, and that was it for the day. Of course, I loved reading people's memories of Scott.

One afternoon, I came across two stacks of cards/letters/ pictures from the children in our Sunday School. Two stacks?

Yes. The week before Scott's death was Pastor Appreciation Sunday, and the kids had written notes to Pastor Scott and drawn pictures for him. The next Sunday, they were drawing and writing cards of sympathy to me.

Of course, children have only a hazy understanding of what is happening in regard to death, and most of them would not have known Scott personally, but I spent an entire afternoon laughing and crying over the sweet things they wrote. They drew pictures of Scott playing football with NFL angels in heaven. He was skateboarding, roller-blading, eating, and going to a heavenly version of Chuck E. Cheese's. (I guess this gives us an idea of what they think are "heavenly" things!) They spelled his name every possible way: Scoot, Scout, Scott.

One favorite was from my nephew, who was nine years old at the time. He drew a picture of Scott, but without glasses. At the bottom of the picture, he included a note to make sure I understood that this was not an oversight: *"In heaven, Uncle Scott won't need glasses anymore."*

The paper process was very labor intensive, because everything had to be gone through. I had to go through his desk at home, too, because I was now responsible for all of that. But in the process there were some sweet surprises. One thing I discovered was that he had already purchased Mother's Day cards for both me and his mom for the following year! I'm sure he was just trying to plan ahead, but it was a loving surprise to receive one more card from him.

Interaction: Dealing with the Stuff, Part 2

Immediate Choices

There were several things I felt the need to do immediately. The things that fall into this category will be different for everyone. They may or may not be directly related to the loved one who has passed away, but they are decisions that give an outward acknowledgment that life has changed. One widow told me that she went out and bought a different perfume, because she had worn "that one" whenever she and her husband went out somewhere special. She needed a different scent surrounding her now. Another had her car painted a different color. There isn't a right or wrong answer to this. It's simply a tangible way of acknowledging a gigantic life change. Whatever that life change is for you, there is a way—via keeping, discarding or altering something—that allows you to boldly (even if it doesn't feel bold) acknowledge that change and take a step toward your future.

One of the things that were important to me was to bring something home from Scott's office. He had a shepherd's staff that represented his life call. I wanted it at home immediately because it represented several things to me. First, it reminded me that Jesus was my shepherd, and His rod and His staff would comfort me. It also represented *my* life calling . . . and the fact that now I was taking that call up at a different dimension. Third, it spoke to the direction I was heading: I was following the Good Shepherd.

Make an immediate decision that is important to you.

Stuff Comes Off in Layers, Too

You don't think about these things until you have to, but I think I always figured that you would go through someone's personal effects once and be done with the task. But over time, I discovered that the things actually came off in layers. As I processed my layers of grief, the layers of things got processed as well. You may want to have a moral support person with you for some of the significant letting-go-of-things moments.

In the initial process, I decided to "keep anything that gave me comfort." I kept a lot. The next time I went through all of the things was several years later. Then it was about once a year for several years, until I felt that it was probably the last time. But . . . that was my journey. Yours may look different. The point is, in the initial stages, it's okay to keep the things that give you comfort; you don't have to make all the decisions immediately.

As layers came off, I recognized that there were things that had initially given me comfort but now needed to go. Again—this was a long time down the road. For example, initially I kept Scott's travel bag. It seemed so personal that I just couldn't bring myself to get rid of it. About five years later, I rediscovered it. Honestly, I had forgotten that I had kept it. At that point (for me anyway), it seemed like clinging to the old life to continue to keep it. This was another phase of letting go.

What to Keep, What to Let Go

About six months after Scott passed away, I moved to a house that was literally half the size of my old one. That forced me to make a lot of decisions about things. I found that things naturally divided themselves into three general categories: (1) There were things that I just really liked—this could have been a 39-cent item from Big Lots, but . . . I just liked it; (2) then there were things that had sentimental value; (3) finally, there was everything else. Did I really need two sets of silverware? In my old life—yes; in life as it now was—no. In general, it was everything in the "everything else" category that left.

Thinking Ahead

There is an appropriateness to giving some of your loved ones' things to other people . . . but this is another thing to do slowly.

All of our children, of course, and all of Scott's siblings received something of his right away. All four of our parents—my in-laws and my own parents, who loved Scott as a son—received something as well. Even in the midst of grief, the Lord gives us (amazingly!) the capacity to comfort others who are on the journey with us.

But there is another aspect to think of as you sort through the things: the future. I set aside some things to give to my children at future milestones in their lives—things that would be "presents from their dad" as well as from me. Since all three of my children went into pastoral ministry, there were sets of commentaries, pictures of shepherds (which is the meaning of "pastor"), and desk items that I thought they might appreciate down the road. I kept Scott's doctoral robe, figuring that the first person to get their doctorate will get the robe. (I think it may actually turn out to be me! I'll just have to have it re-sized . . . by a lot!) Ten years down the road, I still have the pleasure of giving the kids gifts from among Scott's things. It's a very happy thing for me!

Another group I thought about was grandchildren. When Scott died, none of our grandchildren had been born yet. I knew there would come a day when I would want each of them to have something that had belonged to Scott. In fact, I already knew what that would be: I wanted to make each of them a quilt. Since none of them had been born, there was, of course, no way of knowing how many there would be. But with the quilting end in view, I saved everything that could be usable fabric. Think toward the future as you process letting go of the past.

Notes

1. Charles Swindoll, *Intimacy with the Almighty* (Nashville, TN: Word Publishing, 1996), p. 25.
2. From the movie *Pirates of the Caribbean: The Curse of the Black Pearl*. Walt Disney Pictures, 2003.
3. Swindoll, *Intimacy with the Almighty*, p. 32.
4. Peter Scazzero, at "Fall Leaders Conference," L.A. North Coast District, September 27-28, 2007.
5. Mark Buchanan, *The Rest of God* (Nashville, TN: Thomas Nelson, 2006), p. 61.
6. In Luke 16:11, Jesus implies that our faithful stewardship of physical things will release to us the "true riches" of spiritual things. The issue here is not "things," but our stewardship of everything the Lord gives to us.

9

WILL I DREAM AGAIN?

Choices: Will I Dream Again?

Leaving the darkness of the tunnel and stepping into the light again can be a frightening experience! Though dark, the tunnel felt confined and therefore relatively safe. When you emerge, the glaring brightness can make the landscape of your life look bleak and even threatening. Shadows stand out in sharp relief. While it is wonderful to feel joyful again, to see the light, and to feel the warmth of the sun, the glare can sometimes make you want to shut your eyes and retreat into the shade and cool of the tunnel.

In this season, I asked myself, "I've done the hard work of grief—*now what?*"

It's the "now what" that can have us feeling simultaneously excited and scared. New life was beckoning, but after years in the tunnel of grief, I found that making space for new dreams was not quite as easy as it sounded.

For one thing, I had been trying to "get vision" from the Lord for months. (In this chapter, I use "dream" and "vision" interchangeably to simply mean being able to see purpose and goals for the future.) Once I was out of the tunnel, I realized how impractical it had been to try to get vision for my future while I was still walking through the dark.

As I kept pressing toward my future, however, I realized how much choice I had in the fundamental matter of whether or not I would choose to see again . . . to dream again. I was reminded of a person in Scripture who got to choose if he would see again.

Jesus was leaving Jericho one day when He encountered Bartimaeus (see Mark 10:46-52). Bartimaeus was blind, and he had obviously heard that Jesus could heal blind eyes. He could give new vision. Bartimaeus wanted that. As Bartimaeus was being brought to Jesus, the Lord asked him a very strange question: "What do you want Me to do for you?" (v. 51). The situation was obvious to everyone around, and it isn't that Jesus didn't know what Bartimaeus needed. Of course He knew. But He also knew that Bartimaeus had a choice. So do we. Jesus knows that we have to be ready to step out of the tunnel and dream again before we can receive vision.

This story highlights several important facts for us to keep in mind as we decide whether we're willing to dream again. The first and most important point is that in order to have vision again, we have to encounter Jesus. It cannot happen apart from Him.

We also see Bartimaeus's choice in the matter. He could have given Jesus all kinds of answers to His question—answers that may even have been easier. Answers that Bartimaeus may have been able to fulfill on his own. *"Well, actually, Jesus, I was hoping You would come over for dinner."* Bartimaeus could have taken care of that without any help from Jesus. In fact, making the request might have even obligated Jesus to give some kind of response.

Instead, Bartimaeus gave the risky answer: *I want to see again.* This is the answer that only Jesus can take care of. This is the answer that indicates that we are at His mercy. This is the answer—the only answer—that can lead to vision for the future.

Bartimaeus made that choice. Now, we're asked if we are ready for Jesus to open our eyes and give us vision for our future as well. Are you ready to dream again?

What do you want Me to do for you?

The risky answer takes us out of the dark and into the future. Because the future is unknown to us, that feels risky, too. It's scary to choose to dream again.

There have been times when I felt like Nehemiah as he circled the rubble of his city and prepared to build again (see Neh. 2:11-16). Jesus asks us, *"Do you want to see the rubble of your past dreams built into something new?"*

There were times when it seemed easier to focus my dreams on other people—the people I care about, the people I'm responsible for. My children. My grandchildren. The people at church. While those dreams are valid dreams to dream, for me, they became an excuse to avoid the risk of dreaming about my own life. It was easier to avoid the hard work of pressing into *my* future. What did God have for me?

Residual disappointment over the loss may also cloud a willingness to dream again. "Hope deferred makes the heart sick" (Prov. 13:12). We are tempted to look at the past, the loss and the disappointment, and decide: It's too late for me. Our old dreams are all dead; and we can't see beyond the dead dreams to the future the Lord has for us now. The prophet Joel writes, "Your old men shall dream dreams, your young men shall see visions" (Joel 2:28). *Young and old!* There is never a time in your life when the Lord does not have more for you.

Then there may be dreams that we cling to but need to let go of. The prophets talk about false dreams (see Jer. 23:32; Zech. 10:2)—dreams that lead people in the wrong direction. There are things that we are tempted to reach out and grab (or hold on to), as surely as Eve took the fruit from the tree. We are all tempted to make our dreams happen in our own strength, without waiting for the Lord to open the perfect door.

It starts with an encounter with Jesus. Just like Bartimaeus. Opened eyes. New vision. Fresh hope. New dreams.

What do you want Me to do for you?

So, what is your dream? Is there a dream you had before your loss? Is that dream still something you want to pursue? Or has the process of going through the Valley changed your perspective and dreams?

Does your dream line up with Scripture? Is it in line with the way of life revealed in God's Word, or does it contradict it at some point? I have had people tell me that "the Lord told them" they could do something that was contrary to what Scripture teaches. (For example, one man—in the grief and confusion that followed his wife's death—informed Scott and me that "the Lord had revealed his future wife." The problem was that she was married!) So, let me just say, loud and clear—if you think your future holds something that is contrary to the Bible, *that isn't the Lord.* Get counsel from trusted believers and hold yourself accountable to what they tell you.

Does your dream require faith? If the "dream" is something you can attain on your own, it is possible that the dream is not from the Lord. He will always give us dreams that require faith, press us to grow, and take partnership with Him to fulfill.

Finally, does your dream give you peace and confidence? Even when a dream takes every ounce of faith to believe, when it is from the Lord, you will feel the confidence of knowing the next steps to take. If you feel anxiety and fear, it may be a signal that this is not the right direction for you. If you are unsure about the next steps, you may be in a season of waiting. That's okay. Take comfort in knowing that the Lord always reveals what to do next in His perfect timing.

Choose to dream big! Then respond the way Bartimaeus did when vision was given to him:

He received his sight and followed Jesus . . . (Mark 10:52).

Wrestling: As Good As It Once Was

Scott and I had walked the loss journey together when his brother died, and because of that, I knew much of what he would expect from me on my journey without him. We had walked through the Valley with our sister-in-law, and we knew the pain of letting go, as well as the bittersweetness of embracing the future. When she got remarried, it was, of course, another goodbye to Tom. How could you avoid that? But I was so focused on the past that I was not rejoicing with her in her future. Scott confronted me one day: "If you want your friendship with her to go into the future, you are going to have to embrace her new life. It's your choice." Over time, the Lord gave Scott and me such a sweet friendship with Cathy and Dennis, even giving Scott a new brother. When Scott died, they were two of my greatest strengths.

In fact, because they understood this journey so intimately, when I moved to my new home, they flew out to help me. Cathy helped me unpack, while Dennis set up phones and computers, put blinds up, and constructed shelves. I was so thankful!

Now I was walking the road of saying goodbye to my past and embracing a new future. A few years in, light had returned to my life. I felt happy! Even joyous. Sorrow had truly "fled away" (see Isa. 35:10).

One day, I came across a promise of the Lord in my Bible reading: "I will make everything as good for them as it once was" (Jer. 32:44, *NCV*). As soon as I read that verse, my heart leapt as I realized that is exactly how I felt!

Inherent in that verse were some essential concepts for embracing my future. The verse says that God will make everything "as good as it once was"—not "the same as it once was." God is committed to taking us into a new future, not to giving us a clone-life that looks like something we once had.

Nor is He competing with what we once had. He was not calling me to never remember Scott or our marriage or the life we celebrated. He *was* promising that though my new life would be different, it would be equally fulfilling.

For a time I struggled with feelings of guilt over the joy I found as the Lord healed my heart and made all things new. *How could I be happy when Scott wasn't here? How could I be joyful stepping into the future when it didn't include him anymore?*

One thing we can be sure of is that it is "the accuser of [the] brethren" (Rev. 12:10) who keeps us tied to our past in a way that is unhealthy. Whenever guilt or fear or condemnation begins to rise in our hearts, we can be certain that it is our adversary seeking to hold us back from fully embracing the future God has promised us.

Author Francis Frangipane writes:

Longing for a deceased loved one is normal. However, life's tragedies also have a way of obligating us to a false loyalty which prohibits the release of our pain. . . . We must also see that, as painful as the loss of a loved one is, we cannot permit the wounds of our past to nullify what God has for us in our future. Even if we enter limping, we must not settle for something outside our destiny. God's grace is here now. With His help, we must *choose* to journey on.[1]

The choice, again, is ours to make; and we delude ourselves if we think we are the only ones who have ever had to make it. This choice comes to us all. The apostle Paul writes, "This one thing I do, forgetting those things which are behind, and reaching forth unto those things which are before, I press toward the mark for the prize of the high calling of God in Christ Jesus" (Phil. 3:13-14, *KJV*). My task was to keep reaching forward in answer to the Lord's call on my life.

His promise is there for me to embrace and pursue. Scripture says that "there has not failed one word of all His good promise" (1 Kings 8:56). The psalmist declares, "Your thoughts toward us cannot be recounted . . . they are more than can be numbered" (Ps. 40:5). The apostle affirms that all of God's promises are "Yes" (they are *for you!*) and "Amen" (they will be established) through Jesus Christ (see 2 Cor. 1:20). Did you catch that? The Lord promises that all of His promises are for you.

"as good as it once was . . . "

The use of the word "good" is significant. The first time that word is ever used in Scripture is when God creates the world and says, "This is good!" Obviously, we know that after that initial proclamation of goodness, sin entered the picture. But whenever we see the Lord doing something "good" after that, it is His redemptive activity returning our lives to His original intent and purpose. While nothing here on earth will ever be perfect until Jesus returns, He is always relating to us in redemption that heals, saves, restores and fulfills.

- You meant evil against me; but God meant it for good (Gen. 50:20).
- To the righteous, good shall be repaid (Prov. 13:21).
- All things work together for good to those who love God, to those who are the called according to His purpose (Rom. 8:28).

He promises to make everything *"as good as it once was."*

Lesson: Learning to Dream Again

It's really amazing how our bodies respond to stress, loss and trauma. One of the things my body did was to stop dreaming. Literally. For the first few months, I would have dreams about Scott . . . and when I woke up, the entire upheaval hit again like a bag of bricks. It was awful.

Then I stopped dreaming.

It was like that for several years, until one Christmas I asked the Lord to help me start to dream again. He answered me. However, it was as though I really *did* have to learn how all over again! I began by dreaming in black and white. A few weeks later, my dreams looked like a tinted photograph or sepia tone. Finally, I began to dream again . . . in color.

Walking out of the Valley of the Shadow is a lot like that. In the dark of the tunnel, everything looks gray; as the light increases, colors begin to appear.

I've found that a lot of us have forgotten how to dream—and if you've been on a grief journey, the landscape of your life may look completely different now. Learning how to dream again is an important piece of heading into the future.

Despite the fact that I had started dreaming again at night, I still didn't know how to dream again for my future. That became very clear when, at a seminar I attended, we were asked to write down what we saw for our future. Everyone else immediately started writing, while I sat there, staring at the paper and thinking, *I have absolutely no idea what I want for my future.* Even five years into the journey, I still was unable to define a goal or dream for the future.

Important steps had been taken—emotionally, with my family, regarding my job. But the dream or vision for the next season of my life remained out of reach. Scripture instructs us to "write the vision and make it plain on tablets, that he may run who reads it" (Hab. 2:2). To run the race toward the future, I knew that I needed to "write the vision." So, what does "the dream" look like? Psalm 126 gives us some clues.

Describing God's people returning from captivity, the psalmist says, "We were like those who dream" (v. 1). The word used here describes the obvious concept of "dreaming," but also carries the connotation of being healthy or strong—able to walk out those dreams. So the first lesson of this psalm is that sometimes we cannot dream because we aren't ready to. We're still on the road to getting well, and dreaming can be premature. If that's you—no angst allowed! Set this aside for now, and when you're ready, dreams for your future will pour out of you! One of the ways this particular aspect showed up in my life was in regard to school. I had checked out schools—I'd even begun the application process at one—and it all just felt so *wrong*. A few years later, I found the right program, and everything began to come together. Interestingly, I discovered that the program was a new one at that school! When I had originally started looking at schools, this program didn't even exist yet. So—I repeat—no angst. God's timing is perfect. Finish getting healthy, and the Lord will bring it all together.

Joy is part of the dreaming process, too. Laughter and singing pour out (see v. 2), along with praise for all that God has done—for us, on the trip through the Valley of the Shadow; for Israel, on their return to God's land of promise following captivity. I knew that I had stepped out of the tunnel when joy and light, praise and laughter became part of my daily life again! I was ready for dreams.

Two times the psalmist uses the phrase "turn again our captivity" (vv. 1,4, *KJV*). The word translated here as "turn again" is translated many ways in Scripture. While it is primarily used for "return," it is also translated as restore, recover, deliver and recompense. There is a lot tied up in this word when we are asking the Lord to "turn again our captivity." *Turn away what has held us captive, Lord—and now—Restore! Recover! Deliver! Repay!* It is a call to the Lord to do the *whole* job! In fact, one place that this word is used is in 1 Samuel 30:19: "David *recovered* all."

Promise for the future is here, too:

Those who sow in tears shall reap in joy.
He who continually goes forth weeping,
Bearing seed for sowing,
Shall doubtless come again with rejoicing,
Bringing his sheaves with him (vv. 5-6).

Notice the word "doubtless"? There is no doubt about this! God is bringing about the promise of joy . . . and of harvest.

What do you dream for your future? As with every area of life, this part of the process needs to be done *in front of Jesus*. Ask Him to stir in your heart the dreams He has for you. Write the vision. Make it plain. You may start simply, like with the adjective file (see p. 190), or you may be ready to begin writing full-fledged dreams, hopes, goals and objectives for your future. As you do, include the following areas:

- Where do you see your career going? Or do you see a change in career?
- Do you see yourself going back to school? What would you like to study?
- Do you see yourself living where you are currently? What would be a goal in that area?
- What do you dream for your family? Marriage? Children?
- What are some personal goals (hobbies, activities, personal enrichment)?
- Are there areas in which you need to grow? What are your dreams for those things?
- What about your church life? Volunteering? Involvement? Attendance?

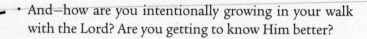

- And—how are you intentionally growing in your walk with the Lord? Are you getting to know Him better?

Dear Heavenly Father,

We lift these dreams before You—the One who is the fulfiller of promises, and the granter of requests. We ask that You would cause each one of us to "walk worthy of the calling" (Eph. 4:1) that You have called us to. We ask that You open doors, pour out favor, fulfill dreams, and enlarge vision. You have promised to "return" us—to recover what was lost, to restore what was broken, and to recompense what was stolen. Now we ask that You fulfill the promises of Your Word. And we ask it in the precious name of Your Son, and our Savior, Jesus. Amen.

"May the LORD fulfill all your petitions" (Ps. 20:5).

"The LORD will perfect that which concerns me" (Ps. 138:8).

Application: Taking Risks

Part of aiming at new dreams is deciding to try new things. That can sound scary . . . and risky. I once read that risk is an essential element of joy, because it challenges us, brings us to new experiences, and takes us out of our comfort zones. All of that contributes to building new dreams and stepping into a new life.

But it's scary.

The challenge with accepting risk has to do with how we define it. Most of us would define "risk" as doing something outrageous, something dangerous, something daring—like jumping out of airplanes, or deep sea diving, or swimming with sharks.

Well, I suppose those would be risks some people might want to take . . . but not me. Some of our hesitance about the idea of risk is that we only define it one way, not taking into account the fact that risk is different for different people.

So, what is risk for you?

One of my risks turned out to be trying new food. In the past, Scott had been my food-taster. He knew what I liked, and when we were at a new restaurant or in a different country, he would taste things and tell me if he thought I would like them or not. After 30 years, he did have a pretty good idea of what I liked, so I never gave this a second thought, but in reality, I had chosen to let someone else "taste life for me." As though 30 seconds of unhappy taste buds would be the end of the world. So, a few years into my journey, while I was on a trip out of the country, I decided to take a risk: I would taste everything that was offered to me.

Guess what? I liked it all! (Okay . . . except for the pickled lemon. *That* was a little intense!) All these delicious foods were things I knew I would never have even tried before. I would have taken someone else's word for it. How much more of life had I missed because I was letting someone else taste life for me?

I took another risk the day my girlfriend talked me into buying a pair of cherry red patent leather pumps. Even after I bought them, it took me awhile to work up the nerve to wear them! Once I finally did, I was comfortable enough with them that I could laugh when someone walked by saying, "There's no place like home. There's no place like home!" *Yeah . . . just click those ruby slippers and I'm outta here!*

The issue is: *What is risk for you?*

I was in a seminar once where the initial question the participants were asked was "What would you do if you weren't afraid?"

The two things that immediately leaped to my mind were (1) learn Spanish and (2) play the guitar. Again, these may not be risks to someone else, but one of *my* greatest fears is of making mistakes in front of people. Both of those activities would put me at risk for making public mistakes, and I was making decisions based on fear. What was I afraid of? Afraid of what people might say. Afraid of being embarrassed. Afraid of unhappy taste buds.

Fear is the main thing that will hold us back from the future. What is it that fear is holding you back from? One caveat: I'm not talking about doing something dumb, or crazy, or that you know to be wrong. On a grief journey, our judgment can sometimes be compromised, and our emotions can be vulnerable. So—nothing illegal, immoral or unbiblical!

The only kind of fear that should ever be in our lives is "the fear of the Lord." The Word says that the fear of the Lord brings wisdom, knowledge and understanding (see Ps. 111:10; Prov. 1:7; 9:10; 15:33). When we live in the fear of the Lord and not just "being afraid," we will take the right kinds of risks—risks that grow us and keep pressing us forward.

Then, define your risk. My risks may not sound like risk to some. That's okay. I still know that the risks I take are pushing me to grow and change; they are forcing me to confront my fears and challenging me to try new things. That counts.

Finally, just say yes. There was a season in my journey during which several of my friends asked me to go do some new things— things I would never have done before. I just said yes to them. These friends encouraged me to:

- Go to a costume party. Don't ask me why, but I would have just viewed this as too juvenile. It seems, though, that

I read somewhere that we are supposed to be like "little children" (Matt. 18:3; 19:14).

- Go on a zip line. The worst part was climbing up to the platform. Don't look down!

- Go on amusement park rides I wouldn't normally go on.

- Participate in The Color Run. Okay . . . we walked . . . and got color thrown on us.

- Buy red heels. What can I say? There really is no place like home!

I've also spent a couple of weeks in a monastery in Jerusalem, learned how to swim, spent the night in the Negev, learned to like sushi, and started a Ph.D. program! I have a list of things to do that will keep pushing me out of my comfort zone. I'm still saying yes to my friends. I'm still growing, challenging fear, and tasting new things.

What's your risk? What would you do if you weren't afraid?

Interaction: What Do I Want My New Life to Look Like?

It was a New Year's Day several years into my journey, and as I was watching the Rose Parade and putting away Christmas decorations, I was talking to the Lord about my future. Suddenly, out of my mouth popped the words "I want my new life to be creative, adventurous and fun!"

I actually clapped my hand over my mouth! Creative and fun, I could handle . . . but *adventurous* scared me to death!

Later that day, some friends called and asked if I would go flying with them the next week. Seriously, this plane of theirs was about the size of a Volkswagen . . . but off we went, and I began to learn how to embrace adventure.

This experience was the beginning of my adjective file: *Creative. Adventurous. Fun.* (The "adjective file" is what I called the computer file where I kept all of this information. Primarily it was comprised of adjectives, though several times I put phrases or nouns in it as well. What I liked about all of the words, though is that they were "describing" words rather than "doing" words.)

As I aimed at a new life, and learned to dream again, I started to define what it was that I wanted. We looked at the external things of life earlier; here I focused on the internal things: who I want to be . . . *how* I want to be. It is easy to get so bogged down in the everyday that we stop requiring growth of ourselves. We tend to be good at buckling down and getting tasks done, but not always as good at creating an internal dream list. So, the adjective file . . .

I created several of these lists over time. I just described the first one, but a journal entry reveals another time I made a list:

I'm sitting in my hotel room at [a conference] (Feb. 23, 2007). This week I feel that there is more that the Lord is digging up in me regarding my future . . . my hopes . . . my desires. I find myself longing for a life different from the one I had. Not because I regret that life. I never asked for a different life . . . but it is what I got. That life was cruelly and suddenly ripped away from me. It ended. It's over. I didn't choose to have it end the way it did.

    I loved that life.

I would never have looked for a life different from what I had . . . but I've been given no choice. I find myself aching . . . yes, aching . . . for newness.

I hardly even know how to express what it is I want.

- *I want youth, vitality, freshness, rebirth—springtime.*
- *I want to create, not just shuffle papers.*
- *I want a life of impact; I want to make a difference.*

It's obvious from that journal entry that there were things stirring in my heart that I did not even know how to give place to. "The ache for newness" is probably the best descriptor of that season. Those stirrings will come to your own heart, too, if they have not yet. When they do . . . start your adjective file!

Two of the phrases I added to my adjective file flowed out of my time in the Word one day. That year I was reading *THE MESSAGE* version, and Matthew 11:28-30 just spoke to me:

Get away with me and you'll recover your life. I'll show you how to take a real rest. Walk with me and work with me—watch how I do it. Learn the unforced rhythms of grace. I won't lay anything heavy or ill-fitting on you. Keep company with me and you'll learn to live freely and lightly.

Freely and lightly. Rhythms of grace.

These examples are given just to get you thinking. Your list will be different depending on the things you want to see in your life. Be bold! Let Jesus transform you into something new!

Here is a list to start you dreaming:

Creative	Joyful
Passionate	Springtime
Fun	New beginnings
Entrepreneurial	Risk
Spontaneous	Kindness
Accomplished	Determination
Energetic	Color
Adventurous	True to self
Vibrant	Artistic
Strong	Hope
Called	Expectancy
Chosen	Inspiring
Re-creation	Insightful
Laughter	Humor
Powerful	Balance
Purposeful	Serving God
Celebration	Content
Compassionate	

Note

1. Francis Frangipane, *The Days of His Presence* (Cedar Rapids, IA: Arrow Publications, 1995), p. 78.

Part 5

THE COLORS OF GRACE

10

NEW THINGS

Choices: New Things

Behold, I will do a new thing,
Now it shall spring forth;
Shall you not know it?[1]
I will even make a road in the wilderness
And rivers in the desert.

ISAIAH 43:19

In certain respects, my journey began about three months before Scott died. I was at a women's conference, and one phrase leaped out at me:

"Everything is new from today on ___."

I suppose that would be true every day; but in retrospect, I realize that this was one of the very first things the Lord impressed on my heart to prepare me for the journey I was about to embark upon. And it is the last "choice" I am going to talk about here—the choice to make room for something new.

At that conference, I had no idea what was about to "become new"—and on the initial stages of the journey, it sure didn't feel new. It just felt bad. Over time, though, newness began to fill my life. But it had to be given space.

During the rebuilding season, there came a time when I felt the need to give some things away. One of the things I gave away during that time went to a dear friend of Scott's, who recounted the gift in one of his ministry newsletters. He wrote:

> I have a friend whose husband died unexpectedly several years back. One day he was with us and the next day, he was gone. He was filled with a passion for life and for Christ. The two were actually one and the same for him. His passing was a huge shock for his family and also for our church family.
>
> About six weeks ago, our widowed friend called and asked to stop by our house. When she arrived, she brought a statue that had belonged to her husband, which held special significance for him and for me. She presented it to me, and I was overwhelmed by the generosity and the meaning behind the gift.
>
> Then, about three weeks ago, I saw my friend at church. She told me that the gift to me began a two-week period where almost daily she was giving other cherished mementos to friends. As she was sharing this, I thought to myself, *She is making room for new things*.
>
> Almost immediately after I thought those words, she said, "I'm making room for new things." It was one of those "God moments."

It wasn't that she was getting rid of junk. The items were full of sentimental and financial value, but my friend just sensed that it was time to take this step. It was in no way dishonoring to her husband who had passed away. He was probably applauding in heaven with the understanding that her acts of generosity were just allowing her to move to the next place God would have for her.

Since Scott's home-going, my life has been filled with new things:

- New opportunities, new open doors
- A new generation—12 grandchildren in nine years!
- New adventure
- A new home and a new church family
- New joy, new excitement, new anticipation

My list could go on and on, but that would require too much explanation of the significance of each thing. Things that may look small to others were of great importance to me . . . like my new ring (see p. 127). Or the story of my "new name."[2] The implications of each new thing were life-changing.

And receiving each of them was a choice: making room for new things.

Job chose new things, too. We don't necessarily think of Job "choosing," because he had so little control over his circumstances. Like me. Like you. But he did make a choice about how he was going to respond to what had happened to him. At the end of the book (see chapter 42), the Lord challenges Job's friends:

You have not spoken of Me what is right, *as My servant Job has* (v. 7, emphasis added).

As we read the book of Job, it is clear that Job was confused by his circumstances. He was in pain. He was in grief. But he still chose to speak what he knew to be true! And that opened the door for new things. Job's response to the Lord, as his grief journey neared its end, is significant as well:

I have heard of You by the hearing of the ear, but now my eye sees You (v. 5).

Job knew the Lord better at the end of his journey than he had at the beginning.

Amazingly, we get to read about the end of Job's story—restoration, prosperity, relationship. He even had his family restored: "He also had seven sons and three daughters . . . and saw his children and grandchildren for four generations" (vv. 13,16). Though Job's new sons are not named, his daughters' names are given; translated into English, they are:

Beauty. Fragrance. Color.

Job's life after his journey of loss was more beautiful than he ever believed life could be again. The promise and hope of "beauty, fragrance and color" is the same for us. The promise Job received is available to every one of us who has accepted the gift of salvation in Jesus Christ. The apostle Peter encourages believers: "As each one has received a gift, minister it to one another, as good stewards of the manifold [literally: *many-colored*] grace of God" (1 Pet. 4:10).

Gifts. Color. Grace.

Jesus walked this road, too. Through His suffering, He has opened a "new and living way" for us all (Heb. 10:20). *Don't you see it?* As we walk that road with Him—*a road through the wilderness*—the colors of grace (see 1 Pet. 4:10), the beauty of life (see Ps. 27:4), and the fragrance of pouring out everything (see John 12:3) are given to us. *Now it shall spring forth!*

But it only comes when we make room for new things.

Interaction: See How Far You've Come!

A friend of mine was walking out of her journey of loss at the same time I was walking out of mine. (She is a cancer survivor.) We met for coffee one morning to compare notes on our experiences. Surprisingly, though our journeys were different, we had experienced many of the same things . . . and we had both come out with a new enthusiasm for life, a new appreciation for the colors of life, and an excitement about the future. We laughed over the fact that for both of us colors now seemed brighter, and we wound up going over to the hardware store and picking out paint chips! Hers were aqua; mine were shades of orange.

Those paint chips became the basis for this last "interaction."

I brought mine home, and I started pulling out all of the pictures and sayings I had cut out of magazines during my time in the Valley of the Shadow. I hadn't realized until this moment how all of the things I had been cutting out actually chronicled my journey. I started laying them out "in order" and could see before my eyes how bleak the beginning of my journey looked . . .

and how colorful and joyous it had become. The paint chips became part of this process too, as I noticed how grim the colors were at the beginning of the journey.

One of the last clippings I added said, "Believe in happy endings." This wasn't meant to be a fairy tale "happily ever after" statement. It was intended to be a statement that I had built where I believed. Ecclesiastes 7:8 says that "the end of a thing is better than its beginning." I'll be the first to agree that the end of this journey was certainly better than its beginning. Building where I believed had opened the door into the next season of the future the Lord had for me. And my collage was bearing testimony to that fact.

Interestingly, not long after I made my collage, I came across a brochure from a cancer support center that offered multiple activities for people going through that journey. They had some great ideas—from exercise to diet to journaling . . . to collage. The description of the class included the following explanation: "In times of uncertainty and stress, images sometimes stand in for words. Art, specifically collage, can help excavate these images, and for cancer patients, uncover clues as to how the experience of cancer might be creating a new reflection of self." I especially liked the phrase:

Images sometimes stand in for words.

Can I encourage you to consider doing something like this? I bought a big canvas, painted it orange and started arranging all of my paint chips and pictures. This may not ordinarily be your thing, but in this activity, I actually *saw* how far I had come. I trust it will do the same for you.

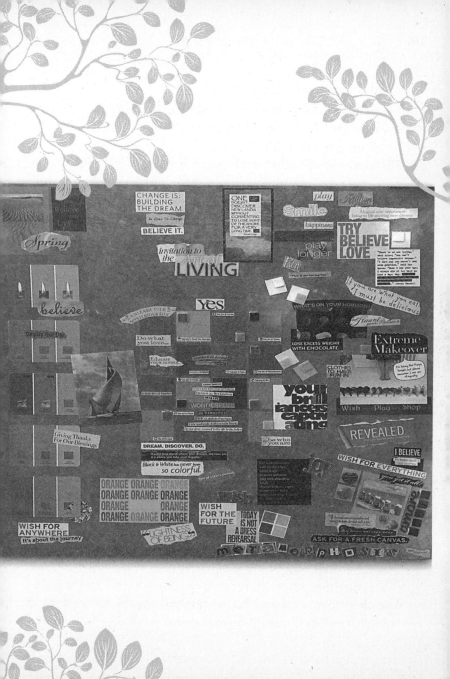

But we all, with unveiled face,
Beholding as in a mirror the glory of the Lord,
Are being transformed into the same image
From glory to glory,
Just as by the Spirit of the Lord.

Therefore, if anyone is in Christ, he is a new creation;
Old things have passed away;
Behold, all things have become new (2 Cor. 3:18; 5:17).

Conclusion: The Gifts of Grief

I shall not die, but live,
And declare the works of the LORD (Ps. 118:17).

This has been a long journey. As you read these words, you may still be at the beginning of yours. If you are, I trust that these concluding thoughts will give you hope and encouragement to keep forward focused. Choosing to walk through the Valley and into a new life is a hard choice that we each make over and over and over again.

If you are at the end of your journey, congratulations for reaching this stage—the place where you can begin to recognize the gifts that the journey has brought you. I would encourage you to journal a list of the gifts you've discovered along the way. We sometimes forget to remember . . . and if we forget to remember, then we forget to be thankful. Again, I'm reminded of Nehemiah 9:17, which warns against not being "mindful of

[God's] wonders." The people of Israel forgot all that God had done for them; let's take care that we do not do the same.

I began this book by saying:

> *I can promise that He will walk with you unto resurrection— resurrection of life, resurrection of newness, and resurrection of a future and a hope. But it starts by making the choice for life. If you make that choice, and walk this road with your hand in Jesus' hand, you too will be able to say:*
> > *I know Him better.*
> > > *I love my life.*
> > > > *I like who I have become.*

That is all true and more! Those are only a few of the gifts I received on this journey. I would like to share a few more:

The gift of silence: Some days, the only way I could deal with the dissonance of the journey was to be silent in front of Jesus. I had never particularly liked silence, but I learned not only to accept it but also to love the gift that it was. *Peace. Introspection. Rest.*

The gift of listening: As many of us are, I used to be more concerned about "telling" than "listening." I've become more patient with other people's journeys, and more sympathetic about listening to their process. *Understanding. Sympathy. Affirmation.*

The gift of choice: The many opportunities to choose that crossed my path caused me to seek the Lord more deeply, and to think more clearly about what I wanted for my life and my future. I feel like I learned to think more like Jesus. *Wisdom. Growth. Responsibility.*

The gift of trust: The Lord has drawn me to simply "believe Him for today"—for His provision, for His presence, for His direction, for His comfort. In Matthew 6:34, Jesus says, "Do not worry about tomorrow." *He will be there. Confidence. Reliance.*

The gift of being happy: As sappy as it sounds, I learned to enjoy moments instead of always thinking ahead to the next thing that needs to be done. This practice has made life happier and more relaxed. *Appreciation. Patience. Slowed down.*

The gift of remembering: Remembering God's goodness. Remembering His faithfulness on the journey. Remembering past and present blessings . . . and already thanking Him in expectation of future ones. *Thankfulness. Blessing. Honor.*

The gift of friendship: On this journey, I had to lean harder on friendships than ever before in my life. Even when I don't get to see my friends as often as I would like, the bonds are established and I know I can count on them. *Laughter. Steadfastness. Sushi!*

At the beginning of a journey of loss and grief, it is unimaginable to think that you will ever be thankful for anything about it. I was shocked when that day came for me. But it came.

Recently I was talking to someone who had a very drastic surgery several years ago. The ordeal involved weeks in the hospital and many months of recovery. For an active person, this was a grueling journey. It meant a loss (at least for a season) of mobility, time and work. As he recounted his journey to me, he said, "That surgery was the best thing that ever happened to me! I am more compassionate and more patient. I understand people better. I've slowed down to appreciate and enjoy life." I've heard this kind of statement over and over again as people walk out of loss. Each person's listing of the gifts of grief is different and specific to their situation—but everyone has received gifts from the process. So let's recount them. Tell of them. Encourage others with them.

Don't forget to remember!

I would love to hear the story of your journey—how the Lord walked you through it, the wonders that He did, and the gifts that you have come out with. Please send me your story at RebeccaBauer.org. I look forward to hearing from you!

Notes

1. Several versions translate this phrase, "Don't you see it?"
2. This story is told in *7 Love Letters from Jesus*, by Rebecca Hayford Bauer (Ventura, CA: Regal Books, 2012).

Also By
Rebecca Hayford Bauer

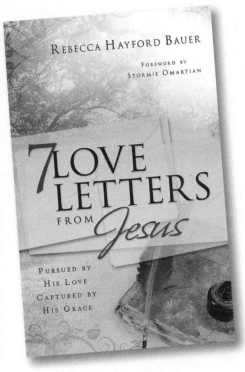

7 Love Letters from Jesus
Rebecca Hayford Bauer
ISBN 978.08307.62187

In *7 Love Letters from Jesus*, you are invited to discover the Savior's love as recorded in the letters to the churches found in Revelation 2 and 3, a passage that paints a picture of courtship, engagement and marriage to the Lamb of God. This insightful, in-depth look at these verses reveals how we can obtain a deeper personal understanding of Jesus' all-consuming, relentless pursuit of His Bride—the best love story of all.

This book is an invitation to be caught up with Jesus now and when He returns.